Excelling in Life

The key Excel® topics students and
professionals need to dominate, taught
through hands-on powerful exercises

WINDOWS EDITION

Optimized for Excel® 2013 & 2016

Printed in the United States of America

First Printing, 2018

ISBN 978-1-54393-907-1

Excelling in Life is an independent publication and is not affiliated with, nor has it been authorized, sponsored, or otherwise approved by Microsoft Corporation.

For more information visit www.excelpro.com

Excelling in Life

The key Excel® topics students and professionals need to dominate, taught through hands-on powerful exercises

WINDOWS EDITION
Optimized for Excel® 2013 & 2016

SERIES

WRITTEN BY
Andrés Varhola, PhD

To my brother Pablo

SUMMARIZED CONTENTS

DETAILED CONTENTS

CHAPTER 3

Math formulas 45

CHAPTER 4

Lookup & reference formulas 61

"

All of us —farmers, students, sociologists, engineers, dentists, stay-at-home dads, CEOs and even some smart pets— desperately need more Excel®, whether we realize it or not.

Preface

It's hard to determine whether this book should be displayed in the *Computer Software* or the *Self-Help* section of a bookstore. Although I'm inclined towards the latter, I can't think of an eye-catching title that might attract insomniac smokers, avid spiritual seekers, naive men that love too much, or those desperate for better relationships. Nor can I possibly argue that Microsoft® Excel® is the ultimate solution to their problems, but —trust me— it can improve our society by releasing us from the tedious and time-consuming grips of tasks done by hand. This is particularly true for students and professionals at any level or career. I also know, in light of recent neuroscience discoveries, that learning a new skill creates magical brain connections whose effects range from slightly reducing stress levels to fully curing mental illnesses. So, yeah, just take a few days to read this book and maybe the sense of accomplishment you'll feel upon completion will give you the courage to leave that nasty relationship, put down the caustic espresso-cigarette combo, eliminate the *"I have no time to meditate"* excuse, or stop buying expensive presents for your *girlfriend without benefits*.

This book came to be through a very risky act of mine. I was asked by the head of the university department where I was teaching at that time to take over a computer course left orphaned by a retired professor. Being then a recent PhD graduate carefully building my reputation as a lecturer, I said *yes* only a month before the semester began without knowing the contents of the course. I soon discovered that no pre-existing materials were available and started to panic just two weeks before the first day of class. The slight sense of relief I felt at the idea of simply using an existing Excel textbook for students to follow vanished when I realized the ones found on the market were either too short and simple or gigantic thousand-page-long manuals. It was then, late one cold night, that after a deep exhalation I decided to apply my own Excel skills and pedagogical expertise to write every word of the student assignments that have now evolved into these chapters. I did have to consume loads of caffeine like the gentleman described above, but, thank goodness, smoking has never been for me.

You should have seen the smile on my teaching assistant Doug's face when he supervised the students going through my first assignment in the computer lab, some of them having opened an Excel spreadsheet for the very first time in their lives. There were no issues and hardly any questions: just focused undergraduates witnessing the magic that can be done with that fabulous piece of software. Then came assignment 2, assignments 3, 4, 5, 6, 7 and 8, all created week by week and sometimes published at dawn before each lab session. At the end, student evaluations for the course were great, like this: *"For some people like myself, computers are super intimidating and [the Professor's] step by step instructions were SO APPRECIATED for the labs"*. Or this one: *"At the beginning of the term I thought it would be my least favorite class, [but] it turned into a tie for my favorite with another class. The information that was conveyed to us by the instructor [...] I will probably always be able to utilize in the future."*

After happily confirming that my risky venture teaching this course was successful, however, I found myself thinking about the bigger picture of our educational system. It is my humble but strong opinion that **every high school student should graduate proficient in Excel**, and that colleges and universities should not be burdened with the task of teaching it. If you are president of a country or an autonomous territory, even if it is an abandoned oil platform in the middle of the ocean, please talk to your Education Minister about making this a mandate!

My desire is that you find this small publication life-changing. Some people, like the students I mentioned, are fearful of computers in general and thus sabotage their chances of performing miracles with spreadsheets throughout their professional and personal lives. With its step-by-step, user-friendly, color-coded approach and candid style, this book promises thoughtful behind-the-scenes teaching techniques and easy-to-follow instructions, even for the most distracted.

Who can use this book?

The simplest of answers is EVERYONE! If you are an undergraduate student in any career, including the arts and social sciences, are you not always going to be exposed to some sort of data processing or graph creation? If you decide to sell necklaces on a tropical beach as a living, it will help you keep track of sales. If you are a high-profile CEO in a multinational, you certainly need to make some independent calculations to confirm for yourself that the company is doing well. If you are a small business owner, I cannot emphasize the importance of Excel enough: there is no money to hire a software developer and no program in the market that fulfills your company's requirements. Excel can also be used in every-day life. A simple database of who owes you money or a personalized spreadsheet to plan your monthly budget and track your expenses may contribute positively to your quality of life. Before you say, "but wait, my cellphone apps can do those things", know that Excel's functions and capabilities are irreplaceable as far as personalized data processing is concerned.

This book can serve people who have never used Excel before, but will not bore someone who works with the program frequently. You do not need any prior computer knowledge besides *double-click* opens a file and Excel is found somewhere in the *Start* menu. Just some basic high-school level math skills are necessary. I can guarantee that after completing these instructions one by one, you will become an advanced Excel user and feel much more confident about your professional capabilities. This book was particularly written with high school or undergraduate students and small business owners in mind, but can touch the lives of all humans equally.

Why this book is unique

There are literally hundreds of great Excel books, blogs and online courses available. However, most of them focus on isolated tips and tricks to achieve specific goals. An Excel textbook may have more than a thousand pages and indeed be a fantastic consultation resource for advanced users. This relatively short book, on the other hand, offers a set of interconnected assignments that, if completed as a full package, will help the reader perform most tasks required for professional or personal duties. In other words, read the hundreds of pages of other textbooks and you will know 99% of Excel but become old in the process. Complete the dozens of pages of this book and you will be able to perform 90% of what you need. What about the other 10%? You will then have the knowledge to consult the numerous other books and online resources.

The examples through which Excel is taught here represent real-life common situations generic enough to be understood by anyone and are all interesting and fun. Through a systematic and pedagogical approach, I will initially teach you exactly how to do things, and then gradually release detailed instructions as progress is made. You will also learn the concept of *Best Practices* —a set of simple rules that are essential when organizing databases or spreadsheets. They help us focus on the bigger picture of what a good Excel application is, minimizing potential errors and making your files automated, functional, neat, secure and professional.

In summary, these attributes make this book one of a kind:

- Advanced pedagogical expertise has been carefully applied in a hands-on approach by the author, who happens to be an expert in both education and Excel; clear learning objectives and specific skills are outlined at the beginning of each chapter.
- It has been successfully completed by people with a wide range of backgrounds, interests and prior knowledge of Excel.
- It includes original **Best Practices** to teach you the etiquette of producing functional, error-proof and good-looking files. This book is not a mere compendium of Excel tricks, but a powerful manifesto of exquisite spreadsheet culture.
- A strong emphasis is placed on demystifying seemingly complex formulas by showing how simple they really are and describing how they work in detail. While some Excel books avoid the use of relatively large formulas, I confidently say that you will love these ones.
- It includes charming and beautiful pictures, a pleasant format, and subtle elements of humor that make learning Excel programming a delight.
- It has **just below one hundred pages** of effective hands-on essential exercises, including abundant images and screenshots! If you focus on completing one chapter per day, you will be done in eight days.
- It includes an optional chapter that will teach you basic statistics like you have never seen before.
- Typical examples applicable to every-day life have been chosen for the hands-on exercises, mostly related to small businesses, interesting educational fun facts or personal errands.
- It is written in simple language that avoids sophisticated and geeky terminology.

Excel is timeless and now for everyone: there is no excuse

Just a few years ago, along with encouraging you to buy this book, I would have had to convince you to spend several hundred dollars on a licensed version of Microsoft® Excel®. Another few hundred would have been required to purchase the new version of the software released shortly after you got the first one, and that you were only allowed to install on one computer.

Brighter days have come. Now you can purchase an Office® license, which includes Excel, Word, Power Point and other programs, for a monthly fee smaller than what some people spend on coffee in one morning. It is applicable to multiple devices and keeps the software versions updated at no additional charge. This major policy change marketed as an Office® 365 subscription really makes it affordable for many more people to change their lives by completing this book.

Making an investment in learning Excel now is also a low-risk venture. As opposed to other programs, which undergo significant changes over time, Excel has remained pretty much the same for decades. Microsoft may improve the layout or add new functions to our beloved software from time to time, but the programming logic that makes up its soul will always remain the same.

Other books and software versions

This book was optimized for Excel® 2013 and 2016 for Windows. Check our website `www.excelpro.com/compatibility` to confirm if these contents can be used with versions of Excel released after its publication, or to understand possible differences. A Mac version will soon be published, and Spanish translations are next on the list. A fully digital version of this book is available at `www.excelpro.com`.

Group packages for teachers or corporations

We offer discounts if acquiring this book for groups. Go to `www.excelpro.com/educator-packages` to select an appropriate plan for students or employees. The educational edition of **Excelling in Life** comes with independent tests designed to evaluate students and comprehensive grading guides for all chapters.

About the author

Andrés Varhola is an Ecuadorian, Canadian and Slovak Forest Engineer, PhD, university instructor, writer and decent karaoke singer. He was born and raised 2,850 m (9,350 ft) above sea level in Quito-Ecuador and lived for five years in rainy Valdivia-Chile to obtain his undergraduate degree. He then worked in the Ecuadorian forest industry, got married and moved with his wife Alejandra to Vancouver-Canada, where he earned a doctoral degree from the University of British Columbia. Andrés dedicated long nights to writing the precursor to this book as teaching material for a university computer course. His altruistic ambition is to see all high school graduates in the world dominate its contents.

Acknowledgments and credits

Very special thanks to Dr. Yousry El-Kassaby, who hired me to teach the course that led to the creation of this book at the University of British Columbia. Dr. Doug Bolton contributed with editorial comments while being my brilliant Teaching Assistant.

My wife Alejandra provided enthusiastic support that became fundamental to the completion of this project. I love you! My aunt Adriena —founder, owner and manager of one of the best schools in Latin America— has made me who I am today and is the larger-than-life inspiration behind all my academic endeavors. I love you too! This book greatly benefited from her more than 30 years of education experience in the form of priceless editorial comments. The writing style was carefully checked by Carrie-Jane Williams, my beloved and unconditional traveler friend. Jennifer Raguž, the best English proofreader in the universe and a Queen to me, deserves the universe itself for her generous help. I can only hope that this book was more entertaining for her than my PhD thesis. My awesome brother Alex sacrificed already scarce sleep time during busy epochs to help me produce the Mac version, but ended up contributing much more to this project. Without Gonzalo Villota, dearest of childhood friends and genius photographer, this book would not look nearly as good or would have cost a small fortune to produce. My parents, Yvonne and Roberto, will always be my guiding light and architects of my life. My children, Anabel and Isaac, are now the ultimate source of motivation for me to become a better human and profitable writer. Love you all!

Cover photo:	Gonzalo Villota – `fotoarkitekt.com`
Images inside the book:	See **Figure credits** at the end.
Editorial assistance:	Jennifer Raguž
	Alex Varhola
	Adriena Varhola
	Thea Beckman – `whybecausesciencebook.com`
	Carrie-Jane Williams
Book design:	Pivot & Pilot – `pivotandpilot.com`

"

Imagine a world where children start learning Excel® at a young age. It would be a better place.

Introduction and Best Practices approach

Most people think of Excel as a plain white grid of cells where you input numbers. After completing this book, you will have experienced a much different reality: you can do with Excel almost anything you want. The white grid will be transformed by you into a fancy software-looking interface with buttons to navigate through different menus or automatically sort your data with the touch of a button. Here are a few examples of what I have personally created with Excel:

- A simple accounting system for my household where I keep track of our income, expenses, health insurance claims / reimbursements, current assets and how much money people owe us. These data are interlinked to produce gorgeous graphical reports of how our finances are doing.
- How could I be a teacher without knowing Excel? Just look at my grading policy: passing final grade is 50%; term assignments, midterm and final exam are respectively worth 25%, 35% and 40%; the exam grade replaces the midterm for students with a valid excuse for skipping it; no student can pass the course if more than one assignment has not been submitted, no matter what their average score is; final grades in percentage must be reported as letters (A+, A, A- and so on). Now imagine having 385 students in one of my courses to realize that I have no choice but to automate the application of these rules with Excel. The magic of one single formula involving a handful of Excel functions protects me from the horror of manually evaluating each student's status. You will apply a similar example in **Chapter 2**!
- A system that kept track of inventories, sales, orders, customers, personnel shifts, financial planning and reporting for my wife's former company. A single Excel workbook became the heart of a small business operation while saving plenty of time and multiple headaches. The main menu of this file is shown in **Figure 1**.
- For my multiple-choice exams in university, I don't grade questions individually. With Excel, I simply input the letters submitted by the students, which are compared to the correct answer for score allocation. I have shared this Excel template with more than one colleague, but from now on I will tell them to buy this book instead. Teach fishing; do not give fish away.
- This book's publishing budget, image needs, timeline, marketing plan and pretty much everything about it were made, of course, in a single interconnected and elegant Excel file.
- Daily life example: my mother and brothers came to visit recently. My mother-in-law and sister-in-law were already here. My brother's wife has a sister and cousin. We all go to restaurants and pubs almost daily. Too long to pay split bills every time; servers are always too busy. I take over all bills to speed up the process, earn rewards through my credit card and get reimbursed by my family members later. Nightmare? Not for me because, you guessed it, I have an Excel template that makes this all very simple.
- An application that predicts possible FIFA World Cup winners. I press a button and the file gives me a complete possible combination of teams based on a semi-random approach with user-defined weights to favor stronger nations. I almost hit a $100,000 supermarket contest prize thanks to this, but my sister-in-law actually won $200 from a betting pool using my World Cup Excel baby.

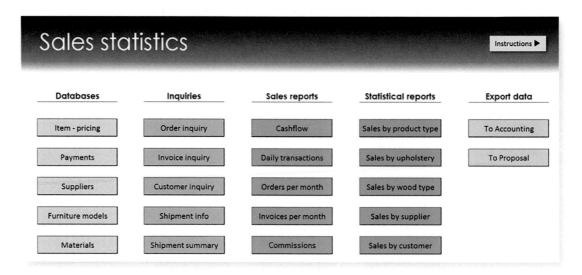

Figure 1. Interface of our company's core software. It was made with Excel and those buttons work! This is the kind of masterpiece you will be able to create after following this book.

As an individual, student or professional in any field, just imagine how many processes you can automate or make more efficient with Excel. I have seen first-hand how, due to lack of knowledge and sometimes fear of computers, people spend their lives doing things the hard way. There is no software out there that does it all, but I am a firm believer that Excel can perform most of what you need without hard-core computer programming skills. I can write pages about the many ways that Excel will enhance your existence but it would be *blah-blah* delaying your process of finding out yourself directly through the procedures of the upcoming chapters.

What you will accomplish with Excel at the end

The following skills will be achieved as you make progress completing this book:

- Understand the basics of spreadsheet functionalities: how to properly set up and manage data, link cells with formulas, automate processes, add marvelous visual aids in your spreadsheets through *conditional formatting*, and much more.
- Proficiently apply the most commonly used Excel functions —the heart of this program. A major strength of this book is how it teaches functions and formulas, and how deep the reader goes to comprehend them.
- Produce lovely, colorful and elegant charts that tell a fascinating story.
- Perform magic with *pivot tables* (create customized reports that automatically change when you change the source data).
- Fully automate your spreadsheet applications: change one input and see how everything else changes in a millisecond.
- Produce spreadsheets that look like software with menus, buttons, *conditional formatting* and fancy formulas.
- Produce error-free and secure files with *data validation*, cell protection and passwords.
- Apply *solver, goal-seek* and *scenario manager* tools.
- Program basic *macros*.
- Understand some basics of statistical analysis in layman's language, applicable to real-life situations.

Much more than an Excel manual...

This book is more than a simple instruction manual; going through these steps will secretly turn you into a computer programmer who creates the most functional, good looking and secure spreadsheet files. You will understand the importance of producing complete graphs and tables, and internalize the principles that a true spreadsheet creator and user must follow. This book is not a collection of Excel tricks, but a comprehensive spreadsheet testament that will guide the rest of your career.

How to use this book

It is very simple: follow each step in order, word by word, without skipping anything. The instructions are based on and applicable to files that you can download following the instructions in the next section.

Download the working files. This hands-on book requires the use of files that are mentioned at the beginning of each chapter or section, which you need to download before starting the procedures. To do so, follow the instructions in the next section called **Downloading working files and answer keys.** Once you start following the steps in the book, save your file with a different name in a very secure place on your hard drive, hopefully backed up in a cloud service such as Dropbox or Google Drive. Losing work in computers is not uncommon and we don't want that tragedy happening to you.

Choose your units before starting. Examples are primarily based on metric system units (e.g. kilometers or Celsius degrees), but Imperial equivalents (e.g. miles and Fahrenheit degrees) are provided everywhere as needed, both in the book contents and working files. The optional Imperial-based working files are clearly mentioned where applicable.

Students only: follow specific file name instructions. If you are using this book in the classroom, your teacher will tell you how to name and submit your completed files. The book suggests, by default, to save them by adding **_solved** at the end of the file name, but your teacher may need your name or student number instead.

Read important background before procedures. Each chapter covers a specific set of skills and includes some background information related to their importance, as well as basic interrelated concepts. It is advised not to skip these sections because they set an encouraging mood to complete the hands-on procedures.

Follow the color coding. We use colors and fonts as a visual aid to identify the following items: **file name**, Excel location (tab, menu, button, dialog box, control, option or cell coordinates), keyboard or mouse button, formula, typed data and procedure number. Important concepts are highlighted in **_bold italics_** when firstly defined and _italics_ thereafter if distinction is necessary, appearing at the end in the **Glossary of Terms**. The description of concepts is as simple and non-technical as possible.

Check the screenshots. As you complete the steps in each chapter you will be able to see screenshots of the expected outcomes, provided for comparison purposes; however, avoid confusion by not looking at them before completing all previous steps.

Track your progress. Tick boxes are available in this book version next to each procedure so you can mark them as successfully completed with a pencil.

Review button icons. Some procedures require that you find buttons in the Excel interface which do not include a caption and may therefore be hard to find. To help you, these icons are shown at the end of each step. Check them out before spending precious time searching for them with your precious eyes.

Review functions used. Ending each chapter is a list of *functions* used. Also, the **Function index** at the end of the book shows a compendium of all functions taught in this book and where to find them. A few formulas have been selected to be part of the **Select formula index** and **Select formula explanation** list, where their logic and functionality is explained in detail.

Request answer keys only if necessary. Completed files with all steps undertaken are available for download as specified in the section below. These are only meant for checking purposes or when the reader gives up trying to complete a certain step —which should not happen often.

Copy some formulas from the eBook. While typing all formulas shown in the book character by character is highly recommended, some may be long enough to justify copying and pasting them from the e-Book version. If you are in possession of the printed copy only, consider buying the digital version at www.excelpro.com.

Once you start, keep going. This book is not one to read and let go; it rather promotes a long-lasting change in your core skills. Some users of unpublished versions of this material recommend doing one chapter per day or not letting too much time pass without working on it. Most importantly, since every new ability requires practice and repetition, use Excel for every task you can think of once you learn the magical techniques here explained.

Understanding program versions and reviewing compatibility. This book was originally written to work with Excel® 2013 and 2016 for Windows®. There are very minor differences between them, mentioned throughout the book when applicable. If you bought this version and are working with a new release of Excel, go to www.excelpro.com/compatibility to see if you can use it or to understand the differences.

Check or submit errata. Before starting your work, go to www.excelpro.com/errata to check if there have been any errors reported for this printed edition. Despite checking a thousand times, you never know... If you find an error, please submit it through the same link.

Request access to the eTextbook. If you are the owner of a printed version of this book, you may request free access to the eTextbook available at www.excelpro.com. Simply send an email to info@excelpro.com including the proof of purchase for the printed copy. The eTextbook platform allows you to copy long formulas directly to Excel and offers other great advantages: scalable text, bookmark capability and mobile-friendly display. Don't regret investing in the printed version, though; it is much more colorful and fancy.

VERY IMPORTANT: never give up. Sometimes, as you complete the steps of this book, a feeling of not completely understanding what we are doing may invade, or you could be overwhelmed by dealing with long formulas. Promise something to yourself: that you will not worry, that you will go with the flow, and that you trust the method developed here with fully proven effectiveness. If there is something you initially do not understand, try to re-focus on the procedure that you are executing or simply keep going because it will make sense at the end. This is a learning process based on repetition, so judge the results when you have completed an entire chapter or, even better, the entire book.

Downloading working files and answer keys

Before starting **Chapter 1**, you need to create an ExcelPro account to download the working files from www.excelpro.com/working-files. Very occasionally, for educational purposes, the reader is asked to complete a task on his/her own, with or without a hint. If you give up trying on one of those procedures, complete solved files serving as answer keys can be requested via info@excelpro.com.

Best Practices

The following rules summarize the novel *Best Practices* approach of this book. They are introduced gradually as you work with each chapter, and make total sense when specific examples emphasize their importance. You may read them now, but each will become clear as you are referred to it in a specific procedure. In other words, don't worry about understanding them in detail before completing all chapters. The *Best Practices* are divided into two groups: mandatory and recommended; they are not numerous but extremely important for the completion of these pages and your future work with Excel. These guidelines will save you time and make your Excel spreadsheets look and operate very professionally.

Mandatory rules:

1. **Never retype values**: spreadsheets are generally based on original *source data* used to produce specific outputs. Only unique source data are formed by raw values and every output must be linked to these data through formulas or other tools. It is forbidden to copy and paste source data somewhere else to avoid duplication and it is strongly recommended to clearly identify the data by using specific formatting (e.g. color fill). The purpose here is that if there is an error with the original data, modifying it will make everything else change accordingly. For example, if you are using a spreadsheet to calculate your mortgage payments and use the interest rate in cell C4, where 5% is entered, it should only be there. If you need to display the interest rate in another cell or sheet, you should use the formula =C4 and not type the 5% again.

2. **Always label and organize sheets**, getting rid of unused or empty ones. Excel® 2013 by default labels sheets as Sheet1, Sheet2 or Sheet3, which should be renamed using abbreviations indicative of the purpose of each; also, never leave empty sheets in a file.

3. **Produce complete tables** or databases that should always have a single header with comprehensive labels, including units for each field (e.g. Distance [km]).

4. **Produce complete charts** with comprehensive legends, axis titles, proper units, correct number of decimals in the scales, professional formatting of symbols and units (e.g. m^2 and not m2 or m^2) and aesthetic distribution of these elements. Always try to improve the look of charts because the Microsoft defaults are often unappealing and impractical.

5. **Be explicit**: when creating tables or any type of label, make sure you are explicit and unambiguous. For example, instead of writing Temp in a column header, write Temperature [°C]. If you don't follow this rule and open your files later, you might not know what they mean.

6. **Create structured databases**: always produce centralized databases with all the relevant information in one single range **where no cells are left empty** (if not applicable, simply write a dash). Do not use separate sheets for databases that have the same structure and share much of the same information. This way your databases may look large, but producing reports with *pivot tables* will later be an intense pleasure.

7. **Avoid formula error outcomes**: sometimes formulas will naturally work only for some cells in an array and result in errors (e.g. #DIV/0! or #N/A) where they are not applicable. At some point while completing this book, you will learn different ways of avoiding ugly-looking errors. For example, you can substitute these errors with three dashes (---) as a convention.

Recommended rules:

8. **Use names**: some people prefer to always label cells and arrays to facilitate the construction and legibility

of formulas. Others prefer the default cell or array labels (e.g. A1, B1 or $A$1:$B$5) to know the location of those cells; I personally use cell references most of the time but highly recommend applying names for specific purposes: when using large cell arrays, when repetitively invoking an array, when formulas are much easier to understand with names and when they simplify formula copying.

9. **Be lean**: exercise your math and logic skills to avoid using too many brackets in your formulas and make them as short as possible; also, always try to solve a procedure with the least number of separate cells or columns (e.g. comprehensive single formulas that do it all). Hide data that do not need to be displayed. Carefully choose the function(s) that minimize the length of a formula.

10. **Identifying cell functionality**: it is useful to identify a) those cells whose values you can change to simulate the effects of those changes on the calculations; b) cells using formulas that must not be erroneously overwritten; and c) original *source data*, also not to be overwritten by mistake. You can use a color formatting of your preference to achieve this.

CHAPTER 1

Getting started: a little bit of everything

1. Introduction and learning objectives

This chapter introduces the basics and ***Best Practices*** of Excel operation and has been designed for users who have never used the program before but will surely teach something new to more experienced users (you may skip it if you are proficient with the skills described in **Section 2** below). I present a comprehensive overview of Excel functionalities and emphasize time-saving tricks from the very beginning to speed up your experience during the completion of this book and for the rest of your life.

The learning objectives are:

1. Understand the fundamental components of Excel: *cells, ranges, worksheets, workbooks* and *tables*.
2. Understand the very basics of how Excel works as well as some useful tricks and shortcuts.
3. Introduce the use of simple formulas and basic charts.
4. Create formatted tables and understand the benefits of doing so.
5. Get acquainted with what we call ***Best Practices***, applicable to all your future work in Excel; they are described in detail in the **Introduction**.

2. Specific Skills

The specific skills that you will develop in this chapter are:

1. **Transforming text to data**: importing simple text data (common format when you download or copy from the Internet) and transforming it into a *range* in Excel.
2. **Performing simple tasks and using shortcuts:** managing *worksheets, cells* and *ranges*; worksheet labeling; column width adjustment; inserting, deleting and clearing; using selection shortcuts (Ctrl+Shift+↓, Ctrl+A); auto-filling; differentiating numeric and alphanumeric data; creating, moving and deleting

worksheets; freezing panes; accessing help (F1); applying undo (Ctrl+Z) and redo (Ctrl+Y); finding and replacing values (Ctrl+F); saving (Ctrl+S).

3. **Applying basic formatting** (Ctrl+1): cells; numbers; borders; worksheet colors; gridlines; alignment; format painter.
4. **Filling missing data:** interpolating missing data.
5. **Introducing** *functions* and *formulas:* understanding function syntax and logic; differentiating *fixed, relative* and *semi-relative references* (F4).
6. **Concealing unnecessary data:** hiding and unhiding columns and rows.
7. **Copying and pasting:** differentiating regular and special pasting; copying and pasting formulas, values, formats, transpose, etc. (Ctrl+C, Ctrl+X, Ctrl+V).
8. **Using conditional formatting:** creating, managing and deleting conditional formatting rules.
9. **Introducing charts:** creating your first graph in Excel.
10. **Using and editing the** *Quick Access Toolbar*: adding, moving and removing commands.
11. **Working with** *tables*: transforming *ranges* into *tables*; removing table formatting; filtering; removing duplicates; creating your own formatting; sorting data (by single or multiple criteria).
12. **Simple** *IF* **statements:** learning the most basic form of conditional statement using the fabulous =IF( ) function.

3. Background

Reading this section is useful but not strictly necessary, so if you are one of those who likes to go straight to the point or has worked with Excel before, just start working on **Section 4**.

3.1 Excel's functional components

The Excel interface has the following components, shown in **Figure 2**, which we will refer to often throughout the book:

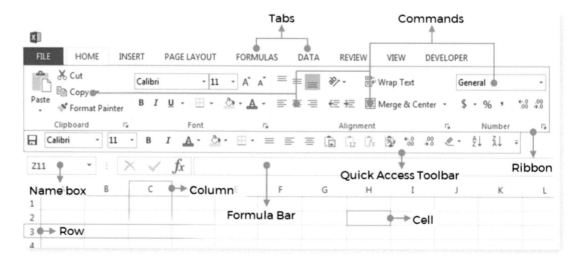

Figure 2. Main components of the Excel 2013 interface (the 2016 interface is identical except for tab names not fully capitalized and a help search utility next to the last tab).

3.2 Excel's basic building blocks: cells, ranges, worksheets, and workbooks

When you open Excel® 2013 or 2016 for the first time and select a blank workbook from the template list, what you see is a grid of individual *cells* arranged in columns labeled with letters and rows identified with numbers; this grid is called a *worksheet* or *spreadsheet*. By default, Excel® 2013 and 2016 include one *worksheet* per file, identified with a tab at the bottom called Sheet1, which contains 16,384 columns labeled A to XFD and 1,048,576 rows, totaling 17,179,869,184 individual cells —equivalent to roughly 2.5 times the global human population. In theory you could fill that up with data, but I have never seen anyone do such a thing for practical purposes. Each cell can contain a maximum of 32,767 characters, so if you fill all cells in a worksheet with the maximum capacity per cell, you will end up with 562,932,773,552,128 characters. No one remotely sane would need to write 32,767 characters in a single cell, so let's stop this. Just one more thing: the number of worksheets that you add to a single file depends on memory available, but some say that things do not work well beyond 250 —way more than enough!

A *workbook* is what we call an entire Excel file, which can be made up of many individual *worksheets*. A *range* is simply a set of contiguous cells that have something in common like, for example, a column of cells containing phone numbers. *Ranges* can be one-dimensional if they refer to a section of a row (e.g. A1:G1) or column (e.g. B2:B20), or two-dimensional if they comprise a rectangle of rows and columns (e.g. B2:H15), but they are always continuous. When data is entered in an organized way using labeled columns and rows for a specific purpose, we call that a *database*. Each row in a database, containing the information of a single subject, is commonly referred to as a *record*. A *field* is a column in the database, which specifies a characteristic for each *record*.

As you might already know, Excel is all about organizing data in *ranges* or *databases* and performing operations or reports based on these data. For this purpose, you can link cells in the same or different worksheets, recall data from separate workbooks, add many worksheets in a single workbook, share data between files, and more. Since no words can describe the magic you and Excel can do together, this book is really about the hands-on experience that will briefly start in **Section 4** below.

3.3 Functions and formulas

In this chapter you will start using simple *functions* and *formulas* in your workbook. **Functions** are built-in Excel operators such as =SUM( ) or =MAX( ). **Formulas** are a set of commands (which may or may not include functions) that perform a specific task such as adding cell values like =A1+A2, or using a combination of functions as in =SUM(A1:A5)/COUNT(A1:A5). The term *formula* is more generic than *function* so we will use it more. A specific function may contain one or more *arguments* that make it work. For example, the function =LEFT(A1,4) extracts the four characters starting on the left of whatever is contained in cell A1. This is a *function* with two *arguments* separated by a comma: *text* (cell A1) and the *number of characters* (4). **Chapters 2**, **3**, and **4** focus on the use of specific and essential functions and formulas, but you will start learning a few in this chapter.

3.4 Inputs and outputs

Excel is about entering stuff in cells and producing stuff in other cells. That stuff, both for input or output, can be **numbers**, **text strings**, **logical operators** and **errors**. For example, you can enter numbers in one column and display the weekdays they belong to in another, where 1 is Monday, 2 is Tuesday and so on (*number to* *text string*). Or you can extract the last name of a person from a cell where both the given and last names are displayed (longer *text string* to shorter *text string*). Or you can multiply two numbers to obtain a result in a third cell (*number* to *number*). You can also type **=1>2** in a cell and Excel will say FALSE —a *logical operator*. Unfortunately, you can also write a bad formula that produces the error #DIV/0! when you divide a number by zero (*number* to *error*). However, you can fix that issue by telling Excel to write a dash (-) only in the cells where the error is generated (*error* to *text string*).

3.5 Transforming ranges into tables

Excel® 2010 and newer versions have built-in *tables* that add functionalities to conventional *ranges*. **Part B** of this chapter explores the advantages of transforming a *range* into a *table*, some of which are:

- *Tables* include automatic filter and sorting options in each header.
- *Tables* allow the automatic propagation of formulas once you type them in one cell within a *range*.
- Duplicate rows can be removed automatically by applying simple user-defined rules (one of my favorite features!).
- Formulas within a *table* appear as referring to the original table headers, and not to individual cells.
- *Tables* provide quick access to specific Table Tools and commands to easily add more columns or rows.
- *Tables* come with a set of predefined color and style schemes that you can choose from (although, as you will notice through the book, I am not the biggest fan of Microsoft's built-in styles or defaults).

3.6 Summary of Best Practices

Please refer to the **Best Practices** section at the end of the **Introduction**, where the general rules applicable to all exercises in this book are explained in detail. Initially the rules may not ring a bell, but you will gradually internalize them as you make progress with these chapters.

Figure 3. Wenceslao (left) and Heriberto (right) were recently purchased in your pet shop by a loyal customer. They look sweet in the picture, but don't get along as well.

4. Procedures

Through the following steps, you will complete all tasks described in **Section 2**, but not necessarily in the same order. Remember our legend convention as you read: **file name**, Excel location (tab, menu, button or command, dialog box, control, option or cell coordinates), keyboard or mouse button(s), **formula**, typed data and procedure. Quick note: Left Click with the mouse is simply referred to as Click.

Part A – Getting Started

You are the owner of a pet shop company that mainly sells dogs and cats such as those in **Figure 3** in three locations: Vancouver, Toronto and New York; they only close on New Year's Day and Christmas. You will now analyze daily customer traffic and sales data of the three locations to get total sales by location and overall, transform the data to a single currency and produce a nice graph, among others (you will see!).

STEP

01

Open file

a. Double Click to open the data file **chapter_01_part_A_sales.txt** available in the website (go to the **Downloading working files and answer keys** section of this book in the **Introduction and** *Best Practices* **approach** at the beginning for full download instructions). ☐

b. The file will likely open in *Notepad* or other simple text editing software, so then select all records in this file with the mouse (or by pressing Ctrl+A) and copy them by pressing Ctrl+C. ☐

c. Open Excel® 2013 or 2016, Double Click on Blank workbook and press Ctrl+V after placing the cursor in cell A1. For other Excel versions, check www.excelpro.com/compatibility. ☐

STEP

02

Column widths

a. You notice that the headers are truncated because the column widths have not been adjusted. Let's fix that: select all columns (A to H) by placing the mouse on top of column A header, then Click when the cursor becomes ↓ and do not let go until all the columns with data are selected to the right. ☐

b. After the columns have been selected, Double Click at any intersection of the column headers (for example, between C and D). Now you can read what all the headers are, with their original units. ☐

STEP

03

Center all cells and save as

a. Select all data again (Ctrl+A at any cell in your range) and align to the center by going to Home tab → Alignment → Center button (when you locate the cursor on top of any button in the Ribbon, its name will show; otherwise look at the icon below). ☐

b. At this point it is important to save your file as a regular Excel workbook. Go to File → Save As and then select a safe location in your disk with Double Click on This PC or Browse and type the name **chapter_01_part_A_sales_solved** on the File name box (make sure Excel Workbook is displayed in the Save as type box, or select it from the list if otherwise). ☐

Buttons used in this step: Center ☰

STEP

04

Format date and numbers, and save!

a. We do not like the date format that appears as a default in the first column, so I will show you what my favorite is: select the Date column, Right Click and choose Format Cells (or Ctrl+1) and in the Number tab select Date and choose the yyyy-mm-dd format. Much better! ☐

b. Select columns E, F and G, where the sales are, and press Ctrl+1, then select Number from the Category list, choose 2 in Decimal places and select the box for Use 1000 separator (,). ☐

c. Even though Excel automatically saves your work routinely, it is a good practice to press Ctrl+S often as you make progress to avoid a dramatic tragedy, so please do it now. ☐

STEP

05

Format header

a. Select all header rows (cells A1:H1), press Ctrl+1 and in the Alignment tab Click on the Wrap text option; also select Center in the Vertical text alignment option. Click OK. ☐

b. Now select the data columns one by one (except Date) and manually reduce the width so that all headers have two lines of text instead of one, with the units in square brackets at the bottom. At first you might only see one line, so you need to Double Click in the intersection of rows 1 and 2 to adjust the height of the first row. Keep adjusting the column width until you get a pleasing view, which should look like this: ☐

	A	B	C	D	E	F	G	H	I
1	Date	Traffic Vancouver [people / day]	Traffic Toronto [people / day]	Traffic New York [people / day]	Sales Vancouver [CAD]	Sales Toronto [CAD]	Sales New York [US$]	Currency exchange [US$ / CAD]	
2	2014-01-02	44	171	58	1,773.02	9,085.85	3,543.80	0.94	
3	2014-01-03	44	118	7	2,036.53	6,323.03	1,415.79		
4	2014-01-04	31	41	75	1,238.08	4,095.65	4,699.99		
5	2014-01-05	79	107	53	3,674.99	5,414.12	2,166.74		
6	2014-01-06	67	0	42	3,812.36	0.00	3,556.65		
7	2014-01-07	44	77	17	1,209.40	3,945.49	1,590.26		
8	2014-01-08	47	48	76	1,698.75	2,698.29	3,250.14		
9	2014-01-09	86	78	80	3,328.76	2,924.18	3,397.46		
10	2014-01-10	69	122	86	3,222.70	4,874.29	4,266.29		
11	2014-01-11	72	72	48	3,031.09	3,550.07	2,133.72		

STEP

06

Add color and
borders and
remove grid lines

I am a maniac when it comes to making things pretty in Excel and hope you become one too because things that look pretty make people happy and turn you into an outstanding professional. A few of the next steps will take care of that.

a.　Select the header row and use the Fill Color button in the Font menu (Home tab) and choose any color you wish for the cells. ☐

b.　Now select all cells using the Ctrl+Shift+↓ or Ctrl+A shortcuts including header and data. ☐

c.　Add plain black borders to all your data cells with the Borders button within the Home tab and Font menu. ☐

d.　Go to the View tab and unclick the Gridlines option in the Show menu. ☐

Buttons used in this step: Fill Color　Borders

STEP

07

Undo and redo

a.　Select the entire Traffic Toronto [people / day] column and delete it (Right Click → Delete). Oops!!! That was a mistake. ☐

b.　Press Ctrl+Z and get it back. ☐

c.　Immediately press Ctrl+Y to see what happens and Ctrl+Z to undo the procedure. ☐

d.　Have you saved your work? Exercise the habit of pressing Ctrl+S frequently, especially if you live in a country where the electric grid is unstable. ☐

STEP

08

Final touches

a.　I personally dislike databases that start in cell A1 and do not have a proper title, so select the entire column A → Right Click → Insert. The database has shifted to the right and blank cells now appear in column A. ☐

b.　Select rows 1, 2 and 3 → Right Click → Insert; three blank rows now appear at the top. ☐

c.　Go to cell B2 and type Traffic and sales for three retail locations (2014), then make that cell Bold and use the Font Size button (both in Home tab) to make it size 14. ☐

d.　Place the cursor just in the border between the header labels of columns A and B (you will see the cursor becomes a ←|→ symbol and while pressing the left mouse button, make the width of column A size 3.00 (26 pixels). ☐

Buttons used in this step: Bold **B**　Font Size [11 ▾]

STEP

09

True beauty is
in the details

a.　Select cells B4:I4 and choose Bottom Double Border from the Borders button in the Home tab and Font menu. ☐

b.　Figure out a way of making the table headers **bold** except for the units in squared brackets (you need to do it cell by cell within the Formula Bar), so that your database looks like this (with your own color): ☐

	Date	Traffic Vancouver [people / day]	Traffic Toronto [people / day]	Traffic New York [people / day]	Sales Vancouver [CAD]	Sales Toronto [CAD]	Sales New York [US$]	Currency exchange [US$ / CAD]	
1									
2	**Traffic and sales for three retail locations (2014)**								
3									
4	Date	Traffic Vancouver [people / day]	Traffic Toronto [people / day]	Traffic New York [people / day]	Sales Vancouver [CAD]	Sales Toronto [CAD]	Sales New York [US$]	Currency exchange [US$ / CAD]	
5	2014-01-02	44	171	58	1,773.02	9,085.85	3,543.80	0.94	
6	2014-01-03	44	118	7	2,036.53	6,323.03	1,415.79		
7	2014-01-04	31	41	75	1,238.08	4,095.65	4,699.99		
8	2014-01-05	79	107	53	3,674.99	5,414.12	2,166.74		

Buttons used in this step: Bottom Double Border

STEP
10

Freeze panes

a. Explore your database by scrolling down with the mouse; do you experience a problem? Your table headers are not visible as you go down... Easy fix that you will remember forever and apply always. ☐

b. Select the entire row 5, then go to the View tab and Click the Freeze Panes → Freeze Panes option. Now scroll down again and enjoy! ☐

Buttons used in this step: Freeze Panes 🧊

Now that your worksheet looks nice and is functional, let's do some calculations.

STEP
11

Interpolate missing data

a. As the owner of this pet company, you want to know your total annual sales for all three locations. However, first we need to change the sales in US$ from the New York location to Canadian dollars (CAD), since your headquarters are in Toronto. You notice column I shows the conversion rate in US$ per CAD, but there is a lot of missing data (see how you have a value in cell I5 and the next one is in cell I81). Excel provides a beautiful way of filling missing data, which you are about to learn. ☐

b. Select the cells from the first currency exchange value in cell I5 to the next value in cell I81, then Click the Fill button in the Editing menu of the Home tab and select the Series... option. The default options are good so just Click OK. Please understand what just happened, because it is crucial. ☐

c. Repeat the same interpolation procedure so that you fill missing data between cells I81 and I153, I153 and I194, I194 and I279, and between I279 and I367 (you must do it four times without overwriting the original data in the few cells that have it). ☐

d. Once you are done with the interpolation, select the entire I column and format the numbers to display two decimals (you should know this by now but, ok, I will give you the Ctrl+1 hint one more time). ☐

Buttons used in this step: Fill ⬇️

STEP
12

Writing your first formula to change currency

a. Now we are almost ready to calculate total daily sales from the three locations. Insert a new column after the Sales Toronto [CAD] column and write Sales New York [CAD] in this new column as a header (in cell H4). ☐

b. In cell H5, type the formula =I5/J5 in the Formula Bar (you may also just type the initial = and then select cell I5 with your mouse, then type / and select cell J5 with your mouse). Remember basic math and make sure you understand why dividing a value in US$ by another in US$/CAD results in a value in CAD (this is what I call *playing with the units*). Now it is time to copy the formula you just typed all the way down. ☐

c. Select cell H5 and take the mouse cursor to the bottom right corner of that cell so when you see the fat white + symbol become skinny and black, Double Click. Scroll down to the bottom of the database to confirm that all cells in column H are now complete, and go to any cell within that column to see how the formula is displayed in the Formula bar. Do you notice that as the formula is copied down, the cell references change accordingly? It is important that you understand what I mean, so, if necessary, check the concepts of ***fixed reference*** and ***relative reference*** in the **Glossary of terms** at the end. Note that the Double Click trick to copy a formula downward only works when a neighboring column has data; replication ends when an empty cell is detected at any of its sides. If neighbor columns are empty, Excel will go all the way to its very last row. ☐

STEP

13

Calculate total
daily sales and
getting help

a. Insert a new column after column **H** and type TOTAL sales [CAD] in its header.   ☐

b. In cell **I5**, create the formula **=SUM(F5:H5)**, either by typing it or using the mouse to select cells   ☐
    F5 to **H5**.

c. Copy the formula you just typed all the way down as you did in the previous step, so that   ☐
    column **I** is complete.

d. At any point in your work, if you have doubts about Excel, press **F1** and you will access the   ☐
    help options.

Your store manager from Vancouver calls to tell you that the infrared sensor used to count incoming people
(column **C**) has been consistently underestimating traffic by around 5%, and you need to correct this:

STEP

14

Fixed formula
references

a. Change the header of column **C** to Traffic Vancouver (original) [people / day] and add a new   ☐
    column to its right and type Traffic Vancouver [people / day] as its header in cell **D4**.

b. You cannot trust the traffic data any longer so let's add a flexible correction factor in case it keeps   ☐
    changing. In cell **F2** type Traffic adjustment: (align it to the right) and in cell **G2** type 1.05 as a
    number (this will add the 5% missing) and center it in the cell, which should also show a thin
    outside black border.

c. In cell **D5**, type the formula **=C5*G2** and copy the formula down with the Double Click trick. As   ☐
    you can see, the formula only works for the first cell because Excel by default varies the location
    of the formula references accordingly with changes in the location of cells. This, called a ***relative
    reference***, is a useful default for most cases but not here since we want the formula to stay locked
    with cell **G2** while the column **C** cell references move.

d. To solve this, go back to the first entry of the formula in cell **D5** and now press the **F4** key once   ☐
    while the cursor is over **G2** within the Formula Bar. It should now be **=C5*$G$2**. Copy the
    formula down overwriting the previous version. Explore the new formulas in different cells
    of column **D** and see how while the row numbers for **C** change, **G2** is fixed (e.g. in cell **D13** the
    formula should be **=C13*$G$2**). Now, column **D** is showing the traffic in Vancouver with the
    5% increment as indicated by the 1.05 in cell **G2**; however, these values represent *people per day*
    and there is no such thing as 46.2 people per day, so we need to make those numbers round.

e. Go to cell **D5** and modify the formula so that it is now **=ROUND(C5*$G$2,0)** (this formula is   ☐
    shown in the **Select formula index** at the end). This is your first *formula* that includes the
    function **=ROUND( )** which has two ***arguments*** —the components of a *function*. In this case, the first
    argument of **=ROUND( )** is the number that you want to round, given by the formula **C5*$G$2** that
    results in a value of 46.2. The second ***argument***, separated from the first by a comma, indicates
    how many decimals you want to keep, which in our case is 0 (zero) to acknowledge humans as
    whole, self-realized individuals —maybe not happy but resilient and compassionate. Did you
    notice how as you typed this formula Excel automatically indicated what each argument meant?
    You should have seen **number** as the first argument and **num_digits** as the second one (try typing
    it again if you missed this, or place the cursor over the two arguments in your typed formula).

f. Propagate the new formula of cell **D5** all the way down in the column. Congratulations! You   ☐
    have now performed one of the most important tasks in Excel, which is to set up your worksheet
    to respond to changes of a specific user-defined parameter —in our case the traffic correction
    factor located in cell **G2**. You also learned what a ***fixed reference*** is!

g. Now go to cell **G2** and change the value to 1.07, then to 1.5, then to 10, and see what happens   ☐
    to all the values in column **D**. This is absolute magic and the essence of a spreadsheet!

h. Your intuition was correct! Your store manager calls again to say that the traffic was being   ☐
    underestimated by 6%, so change the value in cell **G2** to reflect this and leave it like that. It is
    now so easy to change the values of the entire column and your store manager can call as many
    times as he likes.

i. **Ctrl+S**.   ☐

STEP
15

Understanding functions in detail

An advantage of Excel's programming language is that built-in functions are named with intuitive terms and plenty of help is available to understand them. Let me show you:

a. Go to cell D5 and locate the cursor within the ROUND text in the Formula Bar; you can see that below the Formula Bar Excel displays the function structure as ROUND(number, num_digits). If you move the cursor over the ROUND part of that text, it will become a blue hyperlink: please Click on it now. You will now access help for that specific function, where it is explained in detail. Please read it and notice how related functions are suggested and excellent examples shown at the end. Every function comes with this sort of explanation so once you start working with Excel it is very easy to learn new functions on your own. ☐

b. Go to cell J5 and repeat the same procedure as above to read the help for the =SUM( ) function. ☐

c. Go back to cell D5 and Click on the typed formula within the Formula Bar as if you were to edit it; notice how cells that are being used by the formula are color-coded and highlighted (cell C5 appears blue and cell G2 appears red). Now try to move the cell references used by the formula with the mouse instead of retyping them, but make sure you leave the formula as it was in the beginning (or just press Ctrl+Z after playing with this). ☐

There are many more tricks that we will learn about functions and formulas in the next three chapters, so the examples above are just the tip of the iceberg.

Just so that we are on the same page before proceeding, make sure the top of your database looks like this (with your own color):

	A	B	C	D	E	F	G	H	I	J	K	L	M
1													
2		Traffic and sales for three retail locations (2014)				Traffic adjustment:	1.06						
3													
4		Date	Traffic Vancouver (original) [people / day]	Traffic Vancouver [people / day]	Traffic Toronto [people / day]	Traffic New York [people / day]	Sales Vancouver [CAD]	Sales Toronto [CAD]	Sales New York [CAD]	TOTAL sales [CAD]	Sales New York [US$]	Currency exchange [US$ / CAD]	
5		2014-01-02	44	47	171	58	1,773.02	9,085.85	3,770.00	14,628.87	3,543.80	0.94	
6		2014-01-03	44	47	118	7	2,036.53	6,323.03	1,507.21	9,866.77	1,415.79	0.94	
7		2014-01-04	31	33	41	75	1,238.08	4,095.65	5,007.00	10,340.73	4,699.99	0.94	
8		2014-01-05	79	84	107	53	3,674.99	5,414.12	2,309.89	11,399.00	2,166.74	0.94	
9		2014-01-06	67	71	0	42	3,812.36	0.00	3,794.29	7,606.65	3,556.65	0.94	

STEP
16

Semi-relative references

So far, your database shows daily values for traffic and sales for the year 2014, but it would be great to get some overall annual statistics through the next following steps, which will also show you how to type formulas using *semi-relative cell references* so that their propagation in adjacent columns is done with a single, efficient mouse movement.

a. Select the entire rows 4 to 7 with the mouse, then Right Click → Insert. ☐

b. Type Average: in cell B4, Maximum: in cell B5 and Minimum: in cell B6. ☐

c. Select cells C4:L6, press Ctrl+1 → Border tab, select the first thin dotted line from the Style menu, Click on the Outline and Inside buttons under Presets, and Click OK. You see where this is going: we will calculate averages, maximums and minimums for all the variables. ☐

d. In cell C4, create formula =AVERAGE(C9:C371) by typing the =AVERAGE(part first and then selecting cells C9:C371 with the mouse before typing the ending) and pressing Enter. A trick to do this without scrolling manually with the mouse all the way down until you visually see the end of your database is to select a few cells first (say, C9:C12), and then immediately press Ctrl+Shift+↓ . Press Enter once you have finished creating this formula. ☐

e. Select cells C4:L6 again and use the Home → Alignment → Center button to center the contents of these cells; also use the Home → Number → Decrease Decimal button to make them appear with only one decimal. For convenience, we have pre-set their formatting before filling cells with formulas. ☐

The idea behind the steps that follow is to type the formula in cell C4 in a way that will minimize the number of steps and time taken to fill the rest of the Average, Maximum and Minimum cells:

f.   Edit the formula in cell C4 by selecting the C9:C371 part of it within the Formula Bar and pressing F4 until the formula becomes **=AVERAGE(C$9:C$371)** (you may also manually type the $ symbol with the keyboard, but I want you to exercise the use of F4) (this formula is shown in the **Select formula index** at the end). The $ sign just before the numbers means that if you copy the formula down, row references will stay fixed, but if you copy the formula to the right or left, column references will change. You will see how that is useful in the next two procedures.   ☐

g.   Select cell C4 and propagate its formula to cells C5 and C6. The result is identical formulas and identical values (49.7) because the row references were fixed. Now edit the formula in cell C5 by replacing **AVERAGE** with **MAX**, and do the same for cell C6 using **MIN**.   ☐

h.   Now we are ready to propagate all the formulas to the right! Select cells C4:C6 with the mouse and copy them until you reach column L. Wow!!! That was quick! Now explore the formula contents in these cells and make sure you understand what we just did. To summarize it, we fixed the row references so that we can initially copy the formulas down and then simply change the function to be used (by leaving the column references without a $ sign, we were able to copy the formulas to the right). This is what we call ***semirelative cell references***, where we combine both *relative* and *fixed* references in a single formula so that its propagation is easy and efficient. When creating formulas, think in advance about how you will copy them onto the worksheet to determine what type of references you need; plenty of time can be saved by carefully doing this every time.   ☐

i.   You notice that the one decimal formatting we chose for cells C4:L6 is not good for all of these variables, so format cells C4:F6 to appear with no decimals (do not use any function to round the numbers, just format them to hide the decimals). Format cells G4:K6 to appear with two decimals and thousand separators, and cells L4:L6 with two decimals.   ☐

j.   Select the entire row 7 and insert a new row there, type TOTAL: in cell B7 and do whatever you need to do to fill cells C7:L7 with the totals for all columns (e.g. total sum of number of people that walked into your stores and total annual sales). What funcion do you think is appropriate for this? (hint: you have used it already). Also, use the same border style for this new row 7 to keep your spreadsheet beautiful.   ☐

k.   Select cells C7:K7 and format them so that they all appear **bold**, with no decimals and a thousand separator. Also, if you got a total for cell L7 you will immediately notice how that number is meaningless, so replace it with a dash (when you type a dash Excel thinks you are starting to write a formula, so just type it in cell L7 and press Enter immediately to avoid any issues).   ☐

Buttons used in this step: Center ☰   Decrease Decimal .00→.0

The top of your database should now look like this, with identical values:

	B	C	D	E	F	G	H	I	J	K	L	M
1												
2	Traffic and sales for three retail locations (2014)				Traffic adjustment:	1.06						
3												
4	Average:	50	53	86	59	2,488.51	4,238.04	3,320.62	10,047.17	3,003.42	0.90	
5	Maximum:	128	136	226	133	7,528.60	12,978.60	7,162.64	27,669.84	6,172.08	0.94	
6	Minimum:	0	0	0	0	0.00	0.00	0.00	2,160.96	0.00	0.86	
7	TOTAL:	18,023	19,113	31,147	21,493	903,328	1,538,410	1,205,385	3,647,122	1,090,243	-	
8												
9	Date	Traffic Vancouver (original) [people / day]	Traffic Vancouver [people / day]	Traffic Toronto [people / day]	Traffic New York [people / day]	Sales Vancouver [CAD]	Sales Toronto [CAD]	Sales New York [CAD]	TOTAL sales [CAD]	Sales New York [US$]	Currency exchange [US$ / CAD]	
10	2014-01-02	44	47	171	58	1,773.02	9,085.85	3,770.00	14,628.87	3,543.80	0.94	
11	2014-01-03	44	47	118	7	2,036.53	6,323.03	1,507.21	9,866.77	1,415.79	0.94	
12	2014-01-04	31	33	41	75	1,238.08	4,095.65	5,007.00	10,340.73	4,699.99	0.94	
13	2014-01-05	79	84	107	53	3,674.99	5,414.12	2,309.89	11,399.00	2,166.74	0.94	

STEP
17
What about total traffic

a. Insert a column to the right of column F and in cell G9 of this new column type TOTAL traffic [people / day]; then immediately cut (Ctrl+X) and paste (Ctrl+V) the content of cell F2 to cell G2.

b. Type a formula in cell G10 that would add the traffic of all three locations (make sure you do not double-count Vancouver!) and propagate it to fill all records below.

c. Fill cells G4:G7 with the appropriate formulas and formats.

Why not take a few seconds to really improve the visual aspect of your database, which could make your life more exquisite and impress people who see your work? In my experience, only very few individuals care enough about aesthetics (before you think it is not too important, remember how the Apple® empire was built on impeccable design and good looks).

STEP
18
True beauty strikes again

a. Select cells C10:G372 and format them so that inside borders are very thin and dotted (the same that you used for cells C4:M7).

b. Repeat the procedure above to modify the inside borders of cells H10:L372 altogether, and again for cells B10:B372 and M10:M372.

c. Make the numbers in cells G10:G372 and K10:K372 bold. Don't you think your database is now looking fantastic? However, there is one additional step for it to be perfect...

I am very keen on making things look clean, lean and neat. Many times, when organizing databases, you will notice that you do not need to display all the data but at the same time keep columns that are used internally to perform calculations. Through the following example, you will understand part of what our **Best Practices** rule #9 is about. If you look at your database as is, it shows the column for the original traffic data for Vancouver and New York sales in US$, which is not particularly useful. We would like to see just three columns for traffic and three columns for sales, so you will learn to hide and unhide columns:

STEP
19
Hiding columns and moving cells with mouse

a. Select the entire column C → Right Click → Hide, then do the same for column L.

b. Sometimes you do need to unhide the columns to make corrections or see the data, so it is easy to do: use the mouse to select columns B and D, then Right Click → Unhide.

c. Hide column C again.

d. The title of your worksheet in cell B2 now appears too close to the Traffic adjustment: text in cell G2. Select cells G2:H2 and once the mouse is located on any of the borders of this selection and becomes a symbol with four arrows, drag the cells while holding the left mouse button to move them one position to the right (so they now appear on cells H2:I2). Go within any cell in column D and notice how Excel automatically changed the reference in the formula to use cell I2 instead (e.g. the formula in cell D19 is now =ROUND(C19*$I$2,0)).

Your database is now gorgeous and its upper part should look exactly like this (except for the color that you chose for the header):

	A	B	D	E	F	G	H	I	J	K	M
1											
2		**Traffic and sales for three retail locations (2014)**					Traffic adjustment:	1.06			
3											
4		Average:	53	86	59	198	2,488.51	4,238.04	3,320.62	10,047.17	0.90
5		Maximum:	136	226	133	369	7,528.60	12,978.60	7,162.64	27,669.84	0.94
6		Minimum:	0	0	0	41	0.00	0.00	0.00	2,160.96	0.86
7		TOTAL:	19,113	31,147	21,493	71,753	903,328	1,538,410	1,205,385	3,647,122	-
8											
9		Date	Traffic Vancouver [people / day]	Traffic Toronto [people / day]	Traffic New York [people / day]	TOTAL traffic [people / day]	Sales Vancouver [CAD]	Sales Toronto [CAD]	Sales New York [CAD]	TOTAL sales [CAD]	Currency exchang [US$ / CAD]
10		2014-01-02	47	171	58	276	1,773.02	9,085.85	3,770.00	14,628.87	0.94
11		2014-01-03	47	118	7	172	2,036.53	6,323.03	1,507.21	9,866.77	0.94
12		2014-01-04	33	41	75	149	1,238.08	4,095.65	5,007.00	10,340.73	0.94
13		2014-01-05	84	107	53	244	3,674.99	5,414.12	2,309.89	11,399.00	0.94
14		2014-01-06	71	0	42	113	3,812.36	0.00	3,794.29	7,606.65	0.94
15		2014-01-07	47	77	17	141	1,209.40	3,945.49	1,697.71	6,852.60	0.94

Besides being the owner of what appears to be a very successful pet shop visited by thousands of people and selling millions per year, you are now capable of producing wonderful databases in Excel which are much better than those from competitors. So far you have performed many tasks and you likely feel that shortcuts to the most popular buttons and commands will become a source of relief. Your Quick Access Toolbar is located left of the Ribbon, usually above it by default and with only three commands:

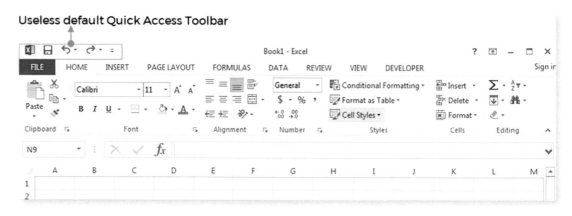

Useless default Quick Access Toolbar

STEP

20

Set up your quick access toolbar

a.   Right Click over the Quick access toolbar and select Show Quick Access Toolbar Below the Ribbon (always more accessible there).   ☐

b.   Right Click on the Home → Font → Font button and select Add to Quick Access Toolbar.   ☐

c.   Add more commands that you consider useful and will prevent constant switching between the main tabs. You may do this by adding each button from the Ribbon with the Right Click procedure shown above, or with Right Click on the Ribbon → Customize Quick Access Toolbar, where there is a full list (it is sometimes easier to find a specific button in this alphabetical list than in the Ribbon). Once you find your desired command, simply select it and click Add >>. I usually like to include the Font (which you already added in the previous procedure), Font size, Bold, Italic, and Font Color as well as the Fill Color button, All Borders, No Border, Center, Align Middle, and Align Left. The Paste Special..., Paste Values and Paste Formatting buttons are needed all the time. I also use the Symbol button like crazy and Clear stuff repeatedly. The Increase Decimal and Decrease Decimal are important because Excel always gets that wrong by default, while the Sort A to Z and Sort Z to A are frequent service providers. Finally, I get rid of the Undo and Redo buttons that come by default because I am used to the Ctrl+Z and Ctrl+Y shortcuts instead. I leave the Save button because it reminds us to constantly save our work.   ☐

d.   While you work, see which buttons you frequently use and add them with Right Click on the desired button and choosing Add to Quick Access Toolbar. My personal experience shows that the commands listed above are the most commonly used, so this is how my toolbar looks (feel free to make one identical for you but remember that you need to do it on every different computer):   ☐

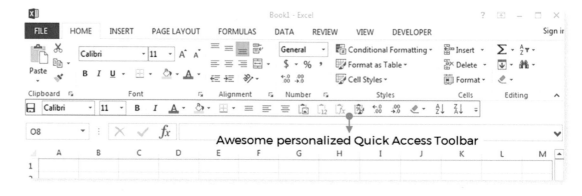

Awesome personalized Quick Access Toolbar

Buttons used in this step: Align Left ≡ Align Middle ≡ All Borders ⊞ Bold **B**

Center ≡ Clear ✎ Decrease Decimal ⁺⁰̣₀ Fill Color ⬧ Font Color **A** Increase Decimal ⁺⁰̣₀

No Border ⊞ Paste Formatting 📋 Paste Special 🖼 Paste Values 📋 Redo ↷ Save 💾

Sort A to Z ↓ Sort Z to A ↓ Symbol Ω Undo ↺ Font | Calibri ▾ |

STEP
21
Conditional
Formatting

Conditional formatting is a tool that adds different kinds of automatic or user-defined visual aids to your data. Wouldn't it be nice to see all days with low sales in red automatically, and days with very high sales in blue? You will now learn how simple it is to create and edit conditional formatting rules.

a. Select cells H10:J372, then go to Home → Styles → Conditional Formatting → Highlight Cell Rules → Less Than... → type 1000 in the box and from the dropdown menu that originally says Light Red with Dark Red Text select Custom Format..., then in the Font tab choose a bright red from the Color drop down menu, then Click OK and OK again. ☐

b. Scroll down through your database and see how all sales below $1,000 now appear red. ☐

c. For the same H10:J372, apply a new conditional formatting rule that makes all sales larger than $9,000 appear with a bright blue font. Then explore your database to make sure it worked; you notice only the Toronto location, your biggest one, shows these kinds of sales. ☐

d. You realize it will be better to show sales over $7,000 to appear bright blue instead of $9,000, so select cells H10:J372 again and go to Home → Styles → Conditional Formatting → Manage Rules... and then select your first rule, Click on Edit Rule... and replace the 9000 with 7000 in the box on the right, then Click OK. ☐

e. Excel has useful built-in conditional formatting options that we will try right now. Select cells D10:F372, then go to Home → Conditional Formatting → Color Scales → and pick the second row first column option (Blue - White - Red Color Scale). As you see, Excel is automatically detecting the range of numbers within the cells and making cells with high values appear blue and those with low values appear red, with intermediates plain white. Notice that by selecting the three columns altogether before applying the conditional formatting, all the values in those cells are considered, making it a bit unfair for Vancouver and New York when compared with Toronto, which is your biggest location. We will fix this in the next procedure. ☐

f. Repeat procedure e but now apply it separately to cells D10:D372, E10:E372 and F10:F372. ☐

g. For any other cells of your choice, explore alternative conditional formatting options within the Data Bars and Icon Sets menu; apply them if you like! ☐

Buttons used in this step: Conditional Formatting

The top of your database should now look like this (I know this one might be too colorful for some people's taste, but acknowledge that educational purposes are behind this):

	A	B	D	E	F	G	H	I	J	K	M	N
1												
2		**Traffic and sales for three retail locations (2014)**					Traffic adjustment:	1.06				
3												
4		Average:	53	86	59	198	2,488.51	4,238.04	3,320.62	10,047.17	0.90	
5		Maximum:	136	226	133	369	7,528.60	12,978.60	7,162.64	27,669.84	0.94	
6		Minimum:	0	0	0	41	0.00	0.00	0.00	2,160.96	0.86	
7		TOTAL:	19,113	31,147	21,493	71,753	903,328	1,538,410	1,205,385	3,647,122	-	
8												
9		Date	Traffic Vancouver [people / day]	Traffic Toronto [people / day]	Traffic New York [people / day]	TOTAL traffic [people / day]	Sales Vancouver [CAD]	Sales Toronto [CAD]	Sales New York [CAD]	TOTAL sales [CAD]	Currency exchange [US$ / CAD]	
10		2014-01-02	47	171	58	276	1,773.02	9,085.85	3,770.00	14,628.87	0.94	
11		2014-01-03	47	118	7	172	2,036.53	6,323.03	1,507.21	9,866.77	0.94	
12		2014-01-04	33	41	75	149	1,238.08	4,095.65	5,007.00	10,340.73	0.94	
13		2014-01-05	84	107	53	244	3,674.99	5,414.12	2,309.89	11,399.00	0.94	
14		2014-01-06	71	0	42	113	3,812.36	0.00	3,794.29	7,606.65	0.94	

STEP

22

Create and
format your
first graph

Chapter 5 is entirely dedicated to creating and editing charts, but a glimpse of such an important task is included here.

a.   Select cells B9:B39 which correspond to the January dates; then, while pressing the Ctrl button, select cells K9:K39 where the total daily sales are (pressing Ctrl allows you to select non-adjacent cells). Once the cells are selected, go to Insert → Charts → Scatter → select Scatter with Straight Lines and Markers. Once a graph showing the total sales data appears, move it below row 10 so that the frozen panes do not cut it. As you can see, the chart has some problems —I am a fierce critic of Microsoft's defaults— such as dates in the horizontal axis appearing overlapped. Please refer to our **Best Practices** rule #4 about making your graphs professional. Let's make some necessary corrections:

b.   Click on the chart's title and change it to Total January 2014 sales and traffic, then change its font size to 12.

c.   Select the vertical axis values, then Right Click → Format Axis... → Axis Options → Axis Options → Number (expand menu at the bottom) and type 0 in the Decimal places box, then press Enter (problem fixed!).

d.   Now select the horizontal axis date values in the chart and in the Format Axis pane on the right, which should still be there, type 41641 in the Minimum box and 41670 in the Maximum box. These values represent the number of days elapsed between January 1, 1900 and the corresponding date, but we will learn about Excel formatting dates and time in the next chapter; for now just make sense of what we have done through this procedure.

e.   Select the Plot Area of the chart by clicking with the mouse somewhere in the middle of any of the boxes within the chart (away from gridlines and data), then Right Click → Format Plot Area... → Border → select Solid line and change the Color to plain black.

f.   Select the vertical axis values, then Right Click → Format Axis... → Axis Options → Axis Options → Fill & Line → select Solid line and make sure the Color is set to plain black; then repeat this procedure for the horizontal axis.

g.   Select the entire chart and make all fonts become plain black (you can use the Home → Font → Font Color button for this).

Buttons used in this step: Scatter 〽 Font Color 𝐀

STEP

23

Adding data
to an existing
chart

a.   Charts should always be comprehensive and self-explanatory, so we need to add axis titles. Select the entire chart and go to the Chart Tools → Design tab → Add Chart Element → Axis Titles → Primary Horizontal. You will see that a box with Axis Title text has appeared below the dates in the chart, so edit that box to say Date and increase its font size to 11.

b.   Now add a Primary Vertical axis title that says Sales [CAD] in font size 11 (use defaults for everything else).

c.   It would be interesting to see the traffic data in the same graph, so let's add it. While the chart is selected, go to Chart Tools → Design → Select Data → then press the Add button in the box that appears → select cell G9 with the mouse to fill the Series name box and then select cells B10:B39 to fill the Series X values box. Finally, delete the ={1} from the Series Y values box (nobody knows why that appears) and select cells G10:G39 to fill that box (you might want to select those cells starting from the bottom if the chart is in your way), then Click OK and OK again. We are making good progress!

d.   Select the vertical axis values, then Right Click → Format Axis... → Axis Options → Number (expand menu at the bottom) and type 0 in the Decimal places box, then press Enter (problem fixed!). By now your chart should look like this:

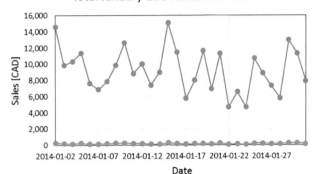

Total January 2014 sales and traffic

e. You notice that the traffic data are not useful as displayed because they are based on the sales axis scale, which is in thousands. Any ideas on how to fix this? Right Click on the traffic data within the chart (orange line and dots) → Format Data Series... → Series Options → select Secondary Axis. Now the traffic data have their own appropriate scale on the right and you realize that, in your type of business, sales are completely dependent on customer traffic as both variables show a very similar pattern.

f. Make the right axis line black like the rest of the plot area borders. Then Right Click on the sales axis on the left → Format Axis... → Axis Options → Tick Marks → select Outside in the Major type box (just to make it look the same as the right axis).

g. Select the vertical gridlines within the Plot Area and delete them (you can do this with your Delete key in the keyboard). Right Click on the Date axis values → Format Axis... → Axis Options → Axis Options → Number → select Custom in the Category box and type mmm d in the Format Code box, then Click on Add. Wow, much better date format for that graph.

h. A week has seven days so while your Format Axis pane is on the right for the previous step, type 7 in the Major box under Units, and then press Enter. Also, those vertical gridlines are hardly visible so please find a way of making them a darker gray tone (hint: Right Click on them).

i. Add a label for the secondary axis that reads Traffic [people / day], also in font size 11 as the others.

j. Right Click on the secondary axis values and retype 300 in the Axis Options → Bounds → Maximum box, press Enter so the Auto to its right now says Reset. By doing this we have fixed the scale to be used, which is required for the next step to make more sense (just do it for now).

k. We have a little problem: how are people going to know which line corresponds to sales and which corresponds to traffic? Go to Chart Tools → Design → Add Chart Element → Legend → Top. That's how! Remember, we will work a lot more with charts later. Your chart is now complete and nice, and should look like this:

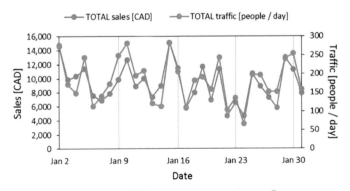

Total January 2014 sales and traffic

Buttons used in this step: Select Data 　　 Add Chart Element

STEP
24

Playing with
your work
sheet

In the blink of an eye, you are now in possession of a functional database made entirely by you which allows data visualization, adjustments based on a user-defined factor (cell I2), and displaying part of it in graphical form. It is now time to play a little bit with the adjustment factor to see some magic.

a. Change the value in cell I2 to 2, then to 0.5, then to 4, then to 0.2 and back to 1.06 again. What happened to the data in columns D and G, and to the traffic orange line in your graph as you changed those values? You have now experienced what it means to have formulas tied to a user-defined cell, and how everything automatically changes as you modify that value. Though this is a very simple example, this is what Excel is so good at. □

b. Now it's your turn! Think of examples of how you could apply this concept of a user-defined value to a real-life situation. For instance, a spreadsheet that calculates your monthly car payments based on changing values of interest rate. You don't need to execute this now; just let your mind dream about the things you can now do with Excel. □

STEP
25

Working with
multiple sheets

a. Does it bother you that your chart is right on top of your data, blocking the view to your majestic database? Click on the circled + symbol that appears next to the Sheet1 tab on the bottom left of your screen; as soon as you do so, a blank Sheet2 should appear. □

b. Double Click on the Sheet1 label and edit it to now be DATA, and then do the same to call Sheet2 GRAPHS instead. Go to the GRAPHS sheet and remove the Gridlines in the View tab. □

c. Go to your DATA sheet, select your chart and press Ctrl+X (cut), then go to cell B2 of your GRAPHS sheet and immediately press Ctrl+V (paste). Your chart is now on the GRAPHS sheet, your DATA sheet appears clean again, and you have learned how to work with multiple sheets. Notice that your chart is still linked to the data in the DATA sheet, and if you keep playing with cell I2, your graph will play along. □

d. In this example we have produced just one graph that shows daily traffic and sales for your three store locations and for only one month. Think of other examples of graphs that these data could produce, and venture to make that happen in your GRAPHS sheet (optional). □

Figure 4. Spoiled pets like this mean a healthy business for you.

Part B – Using formatted tables

The main purpose of **Part B** is to show you the use of *tables* and *worksheets*, although a few calculations are performed as well. This will be faster given what you learned from **Part A**. You will use a file containing a list of your top 2014 customers measured by how much money they have spent in your pet shop. They are star buyers of pet food in bulk quantities, accessories like those disgusting fake bones that dogs chew, and misbehaved pets themselves —mainly dogs and cats but occasional reptiles and birds too. These are people who consider their pets to be more important than their parents or children. They wouldn't even trade their animals for world peace. **Figure 4** shows an example of such a four-legged creature.

STEP
01

Exploring and
preparing your
file and
replacing data

a. Open the file **chapter_01_part_B_top_customers.xlsx** and immediately save it in a safe hard disk location as **chapter_01_part_B_top_customers_solved.xlsx**. Explore the data and understand the information available. Do not try calling any of the phone numbers; some are fictitious, others belong to dangerous felons, and a few will reach telemarketing agencies requiring you to complete a survey (you certainly do not want to contact the latter). □

b. Freeze the panes so that the first row remains visible (you know how to do this by now but if forgotten, please figure it out!). □

c. You notice in cell A31 that Tiler is misspelled because it should be Tyler, and you suspect that your employee who typed these names simply might have made this mistake more than once. Select all the records of the Name column and press Ctrl+F. Click on the Replace tab, type Tiler in the Find what box and Tyler in the Replace with box. Then Click Replace All. Your instinct was right! There were three errors that have now been corrected all at once and without you having to find them one by one. This *find — replace* technique readily accessible through Ctrl+F is very useful and you will probably use it often.

d. Format the numbers in the Total purchases so that they all appear with two decimals and thousand separators.

e. Select columns D, E, F, G and H and center all their contents horizontally.

In **Part A** and for now in **Part B** you have just worked with *ranges*, which are simple arrays of cells containing data. Now you will create a *table* to benefit from all the functionalities explained in **Section 3.5** of this chapter.

STEP
02

Creating a table

a. Place the cursor anywhere in the table and go to the Insert tab and Click Table; Excel automatically selects the full table range, so simply Click OK in the box that appears.

b. Go to the Design tab that appears in the Ribbon when the cursor is on the table and browse through the different pre-made Table Styles; pick one you like but keep in mind that this is a serious exercise, not a circus. If you pick the first option from the Light templates, your table will keep the original formatting of your range (that is my personal choice).

c. Go to the Design tab, Properties menu at the very left and name your table Customers in the Table Name box.

Buttons used in this step: Table ▦

STEP
03

Sorting and filtering

Presumably, you noticed the buttons with down arrows (called *filters*), which automatically appeared on the right of each table header. With them you can sort data and determine which records are shown or hidden in your table. Let's see:

a. You might want to sort your data in alphabetical order by customer, so Click on the Name field filter and select Sort A to Z. Notice a small vertical arrow has appeared on the button, indicating that sorting has been applied to that specific field.

b. You want to browse now through your Vancouver customers only, so Click on the City field filter and deselect all but Vancouver in the boxes below. Now you should see a funnel icon on the filter button of the City field.

c. Get rid of the Vancouver filter and make all records appear again.

d. Sort the data from higher to lower Total purchase.

e. You can also sort data based on multiple criteria: with the cursor placed anywhere on the table, Click the large Sort button in the Data tab; find a way to sort the customers firstly by City (A to Z) and then by Total purchases (Smallest to Largest). Notice again the small arrows that appeared in the filter boxes of the two fields.

Buttons used in this step: Sort ▦

STEP
04

Removing duplicates

Someone could have erroneously inserted duplicate records. One of the advantages of tables is that they can be detected and removed.

a. Click on the Remove Duplicates button in the Tools menu of the Design tab; in our case a duplicate record is one that has identical values to another one in all columns, so leave all columns ticked in the Remove Duplicates box, and Click OK. How many duplicates were found?

Buttons used in this step: Remove Duplicates ▦

STEP

05

Calculating
customer age
and building
formulas from
the inside out

Chapter 2 explores the use of dates and time in Excel in detail, but let's take a sneak peek at what's coming. You will also see a first example of how in Excel we usually start typing formulas that are small and add more stuff gradually to achieve a specific purpose.

a.   Add another column after the Birthday column; notice how your table automatically labels ☐
     it Column 1 because headers must be complete and unique, as opposed to ranges; overwrite
     Column 1 and label it Age [years].

b.   In cell E2 type the formula **=TODAY( )** and press Enter. You see how that function automatically ☐
     retrieves the current date as determined by your computer's internal clock but you also notice
     that since you are working with a formatted table, this formula is automatically propagated to
     the records below (which does not happen with common ranges). However, we want to calculate
     the age of each customer because if they are below 25 it is not a good idea to send them a bottle
     of alcohol; milk would be safer. To customers between 25 and 55 you send bottles of wine, and
     to customers above 55 you send bottles of whisky. So the formula we have now is incomplete.

c.   Edit the formula in cell E2 so that it is now **=TODAY( )-D2** (as soon as you select cell D2 with your ☐
     mouse, you see that the formatted table automatically changed it to **[@Birthday]**); then press Enter.

d.   Select the data in column E (cells E2:E101) and format them to become numbers with one ☐
     decimal instead of dates (Ctrl+1). Your first number in cell E2 should now be in the thousands.
     What does it mean? Simply, the number of days elapsed since today and the customer's birth
     date. That is not what we are looking for yet!

e.   Edit the formula in cell E2 to now be **=(TODAY( )-[@Birthday])/365.25**. The division by 365.25 ☐
     is transforming days into years, with the .25 accounting for one leap year every four years. Now
     the current age of Mr. Upton R. Fernandez is shown in years; depending on when you are
     completing this book, he might get wine! The **=TODAY( )** function will make the Age [years]
     field data change every day to reflect the customer's current age. We are done! Did you see how
     we built this formula step by step, from the inside out? This is a typical practice. As you become
     more experienced in Excel, you will start typing longer formulas in one single step.

f.   Select the entire column A → Right Click → Insert, and make this empty new column A 26 pixels ☐
     wide with the mouse.

g.   Select rows 1 to 3 → Right Click → Insert, and in new cell B2 type Top customer database and ☐
     make it font size 14 and **bold**.

You have now seen some features available when using formatted tables. Note, however, that most of those functions are available for regular ranges too. For example, you can sort data and add filters to any range through the Data → Sort and Filter buttons. However, the versatile duplicate removal, pre-set styles and automatic formula propagation are only available when you use tables. Some people prefer working with ranges only, especially due to the automatic —sometimes annoying— use of header titles in formulas. If that is your case, you can transform a formatted table back to a regular range by using the Convert to Range button in the Design tab (don't do it now!).

Now let's go through a few very quick final steps so that you learn how to manage worksheets, apply more filters, *paste special* and use sophisticated conditional formatting rules that most people don't know about.

STEP

06

A magical and
simple IF
statement and
linking separate
files through a
formula

Did you notice that the Total purchases column does not indicate a unit? That is a clear violation of our ***Best Practices*** rule #3. A call to your data analyst reveals that this is because the New York sales are in US$ while the Toronto and Vancouver sales are in CAD. You will now use the **=IF( )** function to solve this problem. I cannot overemphasize the importance of this logical function because you will apply it so many times in the future! This step is therefore one of the most crucial in this entire book.

a.   Insert a new column to the right of the current Total purchases column and change its header ☐
     in cell H4 to now become Total purchases [CAD].

b.   Open your **chapter_01_part_A_sales_solved.xlsx** file that you worked with for the previous ☐
     step and keep it handy because we will use one of its cells for a formula below.

c. In cell **H5** of your **chapter_01_part_B_top_customers_solved.xlsx** file, create the following formula: **=IF(D5="New York",G5/0.90,G5)** (this formula is explained in the **Select formula index** at the end). Note that if you used your mouse to select cells **D5** and **G5** to be included in your formula, the table formatting will automatically refer to the table headers, so at the end it will look like this: **=IF([@City]="New York",[@[Total purchases]]/0.9,[@[Total purchases]])**. This is the interpretation of what this formula is doing: if the city is New York (*logical test*), divide total purchases by 0.9 which is the average US$ / CAD conversion rate for 2014 (*value if true*), or otherwise just repeat the total purchases value (*value if false*). For example, if we apply this to cell **H5**, it goes like this: if the value in cell **D5** is equal to New York (which is true), divide the value of cell **G5** by 0.9 (which will happen), or else use the original value of cell **G5** (which will not happen). It is of **outstanding importance** that you understand what we did in this step and the syntax of the **=IF( )** function, so if you have not done so by now, please redo this step. Note that we must use " " within the formula above to refer to New York, as it is Excel's convention to identify alphanumeric values with quotation marks. You will learn more about this in **Chapter 2**.

d. Browse through the results you got in column **H** for the new Total purchases [CAD]. Did you confirm how the values in this column are identical to those in the **G** column except for those records from New York? Your formula is working! Imagine if you had thousands of records to be fixed one by one instead of through a simple, robust formula in cell **H5** that operates in one magical step.

e. Where did we get the 0.9 to use as a currency conversion rate for the formula above? Go to your **chapter_01_part_A_sales_solved.xlsx** file and then to your DATA sheet, cell **M4**. That is the value. But why not use that cell as a reference for your other file? It would be more accurate because if you increase the number of decimals displayed for cell **M4**, you will realize that the value is actually 0.904972. Maybe you don't think that is a big difference, but the Revenue Service does for tax collection. Now go back to cell **H5** of your **chapter_01_part_B_top_customers_solved.xlsx** file and select the 0.9 within your Formula Bar and replace it by selecting cell **M4** of your other file, then press Enter. Your new formula will be:

=IF([@City]="New York",[@[Total purchases]]/[chapter_01_part_A_sales_solved.xlsx]DATA!$M$4,[@[Total purchases]])

Notice how cell **M4** of your other file is automatically set to a fixed reference. I personally do not like how formatted tables change cell references to use table headers. If you agree, manually edit the formula to become:

=IF(D5="New York",G5/[chapter_01_part_A_sales_solved.xlsx]DATA!$M$4,G5)

You have now learned that you can link separate files through formulas, but be cautious with this approach because if the file that you are using is deleted or moved elsewhere in your hard disk, the formula will result in an error.

f. Hide column **G**, since we don't need it anymore. The upper part of your TOP CUSTOMERS sheet should look like this:

	A	B	C	D	E	F	H	I	J	K
1										
2		**Top customer database**								
3										
4		Name	Phone	City	Birthday	Age [year]	Total purchases [CAD]	Total number of transaction	Pets owned	Cat or dog person
5		Fernandez, Upton R.	1-161-382-1720	New York	1992-10-15	22.7	4,730.84	4	1	Cat
6		Workman, Lila D.	1-155-875-2843	New York	1957-01-20	58.5	5,149.86	3	2	Dog
7		Waller, Brendan R.	1-129-271-6724	New York	1976-06-08	39.1	5,752.84	5	2	Cat
8		Luna, Elvis H.	1-105-784-6601	New York	1970-07-22	45.0	5,818.91	6	2	Dog
9		Guthrie, Charlotte N.	1-166-775-5394	New York	1981-10-21	33.7	5,991.80	5	2	Dog
10		Kinney, Hector X	1-166-908-1418	New York	1960-06-18	55.0	6,304.99	6	2	Cat

STEP

07

Adding a
summary
worksheet,
applying paste
special and
format painter

a. It is a good practice to keep database sheets separate from other sheets where we perform different tasks. Insert a new worksheet to the right of the TOP CUSTOMERS sheet and call it SUMMARY (Shift+F11 is a shortcut to add sheets). ☐

b. Go to the TOP CUSTOMERS sheet and horizontally select the header cells from Age [years] to Pets owned (cells F4:J4) and press Ctrl+C. ☐

c. Go to cell B5 of the SUMMARY sheet and select the Home → Paste → Paste Special... button; in the dialog box select Values and Transpose at the bottom right. ☐

d. Adjust the width of column A to be 26 pixels and type Variable in cell B4. ☐

e. Auto-adjust the width of column B. ☐

f. Type Average, Maximum, Minimum, Mode and Sum in cells C4, D4, E4 and G4 respectively. ☐

g. Type Summary statistics in cell B2 and hide the gridlines in this SUMMARY sheet. ☐

h. Select cells B4:G9 and apply simple borders (solid thin lines), and then delete row 6 as we only need Total purchases [CAD]. ☐

i. Go to your TOP CUSTOMERS sheet, select cell B2, Click Home → Format Painter and then without touching other cells in the process go back to your SUMMARY sheet and select cell B2 there. Wow, how handy is this Format Painter tool! ☐

j. Now go back to your TOP CUSTOMERS sheet and select cell B4, then use the Format Painter tool to format all your header cells (B4:G4) in the SUMMARY sheet (you can do this simultaneously by selecting all those cells after activating the Format Painter button). Your SUMMARY sheet now looks nice and is ready to be filled with calculations. ☐

Buttons used in this step: Paste  Paste Special   Format Painter

STEP

08

Replacing formula
contents with
Ctrl + F

a. Go to cell C5 in the SUMMARY sheet and as soon as you type =AVERAGE(go with the mouse to the TOP CUSTOMERS sheet and select cells F5:F104 by initially selecting cell F5 followed by Ctrl+Shift+↓ which will automatically go to the bottom of the database; then close the bracket in your formula) and press Enter. If your database were a regular range your formula would be =AVERAGE('TOP CUSTOMERS'!F5:F104) but since it was formatted as a table it is =AVERAGE(Customers[Age '[years']]). In most of the following chapters, we will use regular ranges instead of formatted tables. ☐

b. Repeat the procedure above to get the averages of Total purchases [CAD], Total number of transactions and Pets owned to fill cells C6, C7 and C8, respectively. ☐

c. Format cells C5 and C7 to display one decimal, cell C6 to display two decimals and thousand separator symbols, and cell C8 to display no decimals. ☐

d. Select cells C5:C8, press Ctrl+C, then select cells D5:G8 and press Ctrl+V. You will see the exact same values of column C propagated in the other columns but we will soon fix this. ☐

e. Auto-adjust the widths of columns C to G if needed. ☐

f. Select cells D5:D8 and press Ctrl+F, type AVERAGE in the Find what box and then Click on the Replace tab to type MAX in the Replace with box, then Click Replace All. After the message indicating 4 replacements were done appears, Click OK and close the Find and Replace window. ☐

g. Repeat procedure f to replace **AVERAGE** with **MIN**, **MODE** and **SUM** in cells E5:E8, F5:F8 and G5:G8, respectively (you do not need to close and reopen the Find and Replace window each time). You have now used the Ctrl+F shortcut to replace formula contents! ☐

h. Auto-adjust the width of the columns again. You notice that the #N/A error appears in cells F5 and F6, and this is because the mode refers to the most repeated value in a dataset, and simply there are no identical values of age and total purchases. Therefore, just manually type a dash in cell F5, then press Enter immediately (otherwise Excel thinks you are typing a formula), and do the same for cell F6; finally, center both dashes. Later you will learn how to automatically generate a dash or any other value when encountered with errors). ☐

i. Is the sum of age, in cell G5, meaningful at all? Copy and paste the dash from cell F5 to cell G5. Now analyze your results. See how your top customers have spent more than half a million dollars in 2014. Each customer performed an average of 5.6 transactions but 5 is the most typical ☐

value. Your most active top customer bought stuff 9 times. The average age of these beloved customers is 41.6 years and that makes sense because they are likely owning pets to accompany their children. Altogether, they own 229 pets with an average and mode of 2 pets per family. Most importantly, sales are more than half a million! Isn't this fun and interesting?

j. Aren't you curious to find out if dogs or cats are more popular among your most loyal customers? You will now use a relatively advanced formula to know. Type Cats: in cell F10 and Dogs: in cell F11. Then, in cell G10 type =COUNTIF(and select cells K5:K104 from your TOP CUSTOMERS database, then type "Cat") and press Enter after making sure the formula looks like this: =COUNTIF(Customers[Cat or dog person],"Cat"). You should get 64 as a result in cell G10 of your SUMMARY sheet. ☐

k. Copy and paste the formula of cell G10 into cell G11 and manually modify this formula to count the number of dog people in your database. You should have got 36. Unbelievable! More cat than dog lovers! Who would have thought? It is probably because cats are independent and keep their already scarce saliva to themselves. ☐

Notice that the file is not very explicit about the data belonging to the year 2014 only. We will use this as an excuse to teach you how to modify multiple worksheets simultaneously.

STEP
09
Modifying sheets simultaneously

a. Go to your TOP CUSTOMERS sheet and while pressing Shift select the SUMMARY tab with the mouse. You should see both tabs become white but your view stays with the TOP CUSTOMERS sheet. There, select the entire row 3, insert a new row and in cell B3 type 2014, then align it to the left and remove the bold. ☐

b. Now go to your SUMMARY sheet and see how the previous step was automatically replicated there. Your SUMMARY sheet is now finished and should look exactly like this (make sure you see the same values inside the cells). ☐

	A	B	C	D	E	F	G	H
1								
2		**Summary statistics**						
3		2014						
4								
5		Variable	Average	Maximum	Minimum	Mode	Sum	
6		Age [years]	41.6	78.9	14.9	-	-	
7		Total purchases [CAD]	5,715.08	7,994.90	2,815.66	-	571,507.91	
8		Total number of transactions	5.6	9.0	2.0	5.0	557.0	
9		Pets owned	2	4	1	2	229	
10								
11						Cats	64	
12						Dogs	36	
13								

This finalizes your **Chapter 1**, the longest of all. Congratulations! You are now ready to start **Chapter 2**.

5. Review of functions used

=AVERAGE( )
=COUNT( )
=COUNTIF( )
=MAX( )
=MIN( )
=ROUND( )
=SUM( )
=TODAY( )

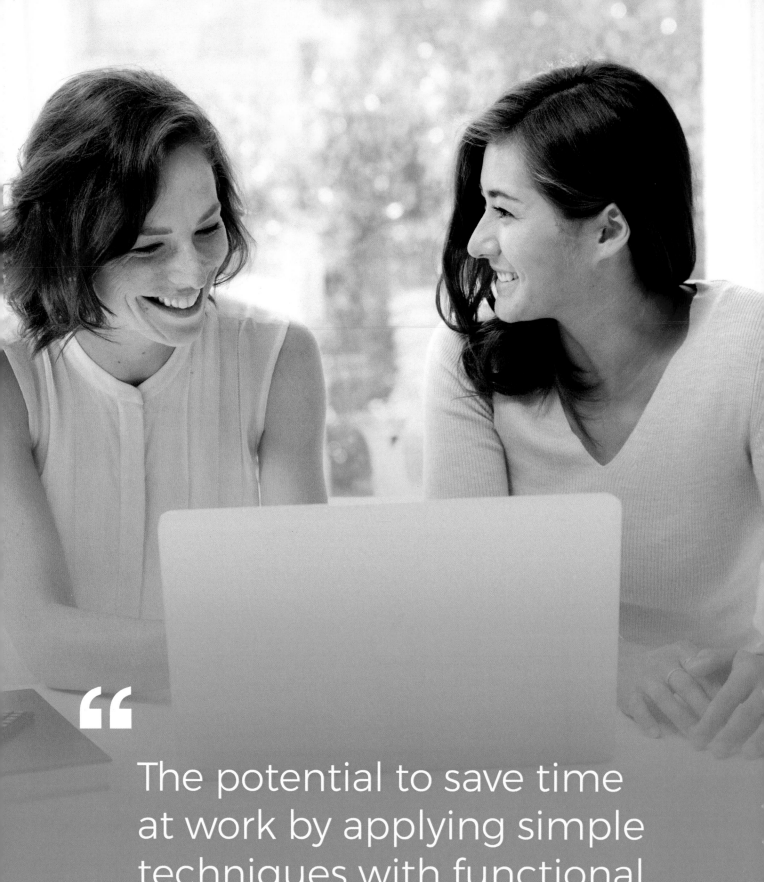

"
The potential to save time at work by applying simple techniques with functional spreadsheets is enormous.

Text, date & time and logical formulas

1. Introduction and learning objectives

Working with text and time is typical in Excel, and is often related to the first steps of preparing databases. In this chapter, you will be introduced to common exercises involving *text, date & time* and *logical* formulas later applicable to a real-life example. You will also learn how to define names to facilitate the creation of formulas, and to apply simple logical statements that we will then use all the time. Remember: as you follow these instructions and achieve the chapter's learning objectives, you are becoming a real Excel programmer and spreadsheet genius.

The learning objectives are:

1. Understand the use of **names** for existing cells.
2. Understand the basics of *formula* and *function* operation.
3. Apply typical *text* formulas to solve common issues.
4. Understand how Excel codes date and time from serial numbers and apply typical *date & time* formulas.
5. Create simple *IF* statements (an introduction).

2. Specific Skills

The specific skills that you will develop in this chapter are:

1. **Understanding what text functions can do:** comparing text strings; concatenating multiple text strings; repeating text; eliminating spaces within a text string; changing case; converting values to text in a specific format; extracting characters or words from a string; substituting parts of a string; counting characters and words.
2. **Understanding what date & time formulas can do:** inserting the exact current date or time in a cell; calculating time elapsed between two events; formatting date and time; merging years, months and days into a single date; extracting year, month, day or weekday from a date; working with hours, minutes and seconds.

3. **Understanding logical functions and their importance:** writing useful nested *IF* statements.
4. **Reinforcing the ability to produce lean formulas:** making long formulas short through better function choices and use of *names*.
5. **Dissecting a long formula, piece by piece:** understanding how a long formula —that you didn't write— works by inspecting its internal elements one by one.
6. **Creating and managing names:** simplifying formulas by using your own names for a cell or a group of cells.

3. Background

3.1 Function and formula basics

Recall from **Chapter 1** or the **Glossary of terms** what *formulas* and *functions* are. Writing simple formulas and functions or more complex combinations of both will become natural to you as the completion of this book progresses, so only a few useful notes follow.

All formulas in Excel start with a = sign and use the typical mathematical operators with the same precedence rules of algebra (exponentiation first, multiplication and division second, addition and subtraction third and logical comparisons last), as shown in **Table 1**.

Table 1. Operator symbols and precedence order in Excel.

Precedence	Symbol	Operation
1	^	Exponentiation
2	*	Multiplication
	/	Division
3	+	Addition
	-	Subtraction
4	&	Concatenation
5	=	Equal to
	<	Less than
	>	Greater than
	<=	Greater than or equal to
	>=	Less than or equal to
	<>	Not equal to

Formula outputs include numbers, text strings, logical arguments or errors that we wish to avoid or change in appearance (***Best Practices*** rule #7).

3.2 The use of names

When typing formulas, you can recall specific cell locations, numbers or text strings. However, instead of using cell locations (e.g. A1) you can rename them to avoid searching for them with the mouse and to benefit from intuitive identifiers that are easy to type in formulas (refer to ***Best Practices*** rule #8). For example, the formula =A1*B1 can be transformed by the user to **=AREA*HEIGHT**. You will learn how to use names in this book and in what situations this is more convenient. This is very important!

3.3 Types of functions

The following chapters will show you the most popular functions and their use in formulas. Excel classifies its built-in functions in different categories, which you can see in the Function Library under the Formulas tab. Feel free to explore those categories and their hundreds of functions. Without functions, Excel would be like a body without organs, pizza without cheese or a car without wheels. In this book we will focus essentially on the following function categories: *text, date & time* and *logical* (**Chapter 3**), *math* (**Chapter 4**), and *lookup*

& *reference* (**Chapter 5**). The chapters focus specifically on those formulas but we use most of them, especially *logical*, throughout the book. Some *statistical* functions, such as the one to calculate averages, are used in some procedures and in **Chapter 8**.

3.4 Text formulas

Most people associate Excel with numbers and calculations, but there are many procedures requiring the manipulation of text with a specific treatment. A ***text string*** is a continuous sequence of characters where at least one is alphanumeric (e.g. *Canada*, *101A* or *Hooray!!!*). Text strings must be identified inside formulas with quotation marks. For example, the formula **=LEN("Canada")** counts the number of characters in the word *Canada* and would result in a #NAME? error if typed **=LEN(Canada)**. To force Excel to recognize the contents of a cell as text instead of numbers, formulas, or others, one must precede the contents with a single apostrophe. For example, if you type **=LEN("Canada")** in a cell the result will be the number 6, but if you type **'=LEN("Canada")** the result will be the text string =LEN("Canada"). Similarly, typing 001 will be recognized and displayed as the number 1, while **'001** is shown as the 001 text string with three characters.

3.5 Date & time in Excel

Excel codes time with serial numbers that represent individual days: January 1 of 1900 is represented by the number 1, January 2 of 1900 is number 2, and so on until December 31, 9999 (equivalent to 2,958,465). The program cannot format time beyond this range. Even though dates and times usually appear formatted in the cells, Excel internally uses this sequence of numbers. For example, January 6, 2014 corresponds to the number 41,645 —the number of days between that date and January 1, 1900 (you can check this by typing Jan 6, 2014 in any cell and then formatting it as number instead of date). Regarding time in hours, minutes or seconds, these are represented numerically as a fraction of a day. For instance, the number 41,645.5 corresponds to noon of January 6, 2014. If you type, say, 10:30 in an empty cell and then format it as a number, it would show 0.4375— the fraction of a day elapsed between midnight and that time. Therefore, when you perform operations with formatted dates or time and you want to transform the results to hours, minutes or seconds, consider that one hour is 1/24 = 0.04167 days, one minute is 1/(24*60) = 0.0006944 days and one second is 1/(24*60*60) = 0.00001157 days.

Excel has a particular and sometimes convenient way of formatting dates as you input them into a cell. For example, if you type Jan 6, 2014 it is automatically displayed as 06-Jan-14 in the cell and 06/01/2014 in the Formula Bar (this may vary according to the computer's regional settings). Therefore, when typing dates, you must make sure that the program is not mistaking days, months or years (e.g. June 1, 2014 as opposed to of January 6, 2014).

4. Procedures

Through the following steps, you will complete all tasks described in **Section 2**, but not necessarily in the same order. Remember our legend convention as you read: **file name**, Excel location (tab, menu, button, dialog box, control, option or cell coordinates), keyboard or mouse button(s), **formula**, typed data and **procedure**. Reminder: Left Click with the mouse is simply referred to as Click. You will soon be so used to this that you may skip these reminders!

Product code	Short description	Detailed description	Supplier
Design Services	Other service	Guardsman Gold Complete Furniture Plan G5C-FR 1703 - Invoice 898	Guardsman
ADV-SG5	Other product	SG5 Leather cleaner	Zientte
ADV-SG5	Other product	SG5 Leather conditioner	Zientte
Design Services	Other product	Guardsman Gold Complete Furniture Plan G5C-FR 1703 - Invoice 887	Guardsman
GINSICOM	Dining chair	Ginza Dining Chair Napoly Grey	Zientte
URAE15IGS	Sofa	Urano Corner 1.5 RA Glamour Chocolate	Zientte
URAM3RAVAG	Sofa	Urano Mod 3 Left arm Glamour Chocolate	Zientte
URAPUFFVWB	Sofa	Urano Ottoman Glamour Chocolate	Zientte
SHIPPINGSERV	Shipping	Shipping and Installation	-

Figure 5. Dealing with text strings like these is very common and Excel is the perfect tool for it. For example, can you extract the last name from a cell which also includes given name? Or create codes by merging letters and numbers?

In **Part A** and **Part B** you will learn how to use specific functions related to *text* and *date & time*, respectively; in **Part C** you will learn about *logical* functions, and in **Part D** you will directly apply this knowledge to a typical example. This is as important as it gets.

Part A – Understanding text formulas

In this part you will learn how to use specific functions that deal with text strings (**Figure 5**). Before you begin, go to the Formulas tab and browse through the formulas in the Text button (if you place the cursor over each formula, a box appears briefly explaining what the formula does).

STEP 01
Open and save

a. Open a new blank Excel file and save it as **chapter_02_part_A_text_solved.xlsx** in a secure section of your hard disk. ☐
b. Rename Sheet1 as TEXT. ☐

STEP 02
Comparing text strings

a. Type January in cell A1 of your TEXT sheet and JANUARY in cell B1. ☐
b. In cell C1, type the formula **=A1=B1** and see the result. For text strings, if the comparison must be case-sensitive, we need to use the **=EXACT( )** function. ☐
c. In cell D1, type **=EXACT(A1,B1)** to do the same comparison. Notice how **=EXACT( )** has only two arguments. ☐

STEP 03
Concatenating text

a. Type your last name in cell A2 and your first name in cell B2. ☐
b. In cell C2, type the formula **=B2&A2** and see the result. ☐
c. In cell D2, type the formula **=B2&" "&A2** (space in between the quotation marks). ☐
d. Auto-adjust the column widths and keep doing so throughout this chapter to avoid overlapping cells. ☐
e. In cell E2, use **=CONCATENATE( )** to produce the same result as in cell D2. You must figure out how to use this function on your own, remembering how to access the help for a specific function from **Chapter 1**. ☐

STEP 04
Character codes

Excel works with a built-in list of 255 codes that correspond to specific characters; to produce a character from a specific code we use the **=CHAR( )** function, while **=CODE( )** retrieves the code of a known character.

a. In cell A3 type **=CODE("a")** and in cell B3 type **=CODE("A")**. ☐
b. In cell A4 type **=CHAR(A3)** and in cell B4 type **=CHAR(B3)**. ☐
c. To visualize the characters and corresponding codes press the Symbol button from the Insert tab and observe the Character code box at the bottom (make sure the Font is set to (normal text) and the from box to ASCII (decimal)). ☐

Buttons used in this step: Symbol Ω

STEP **05** Repeating text	a.	In cell **C4**, type the formula **=REPT(B4,7)**. Let's now find a useful **=REPT( )** application.
	b.	Type Math in cell **A6**, Science in cell **A7** and Economics in cell **A8**, and the following corresponding grades in cells **B6**, **B7** and **B8**: 66, 92 and 88. Now we will create a cute little text bar chart with the **=REPT( )** function.
	c.	Change the font of cells **C6:C8** to Wingdings (yes, even though they are still empty).
	d.	In cell **C6** type **=REPT(CHAR(110),B6/10)** and copy the formula down to the cells **C7** and **C8** (this formula is in the **Select formula index** at the end). Make sure you understand exactly what this formula is doing with its two arguments and why it is practical to include the division by 10 (feel free to see what happens when you take the **/10** out of the formula, but put it back at the end).

STEP **06** Removing spaces		It is common that data downloaded from the Internet contains unnecessary spaces; **=TRIM( )** deletes all extra spaces except for single ones between words.
	a.	Using spaces instead of stars, type ***space****removal*** in cell **A10**.
	b.	In cell **B10** type **=TRIM(A10)** (remember to keep auto-adjusting column widths).

STEP **07** Changing cases & counting characters	a.	In cell **C10** type **=UPPER(B10)**.
	b.	In cell **D10** type **=PROPER(B10)**.
	c.	In cell **E10** type **=LOWER(C10)**.
	d.	In cell **A11**, type **=LEN(A10)** and copy the formula to cell **B11**.
	e.	In cell **C11** use a simple formula to calculate how many spaces you removed in step **6b**.

STEP **08** Converting values to formatted text	a.	In cell **A13**, type 1250.8.
	b.	In cell **B13**, type **=TEXT(A13,"$#,##0.00")**.
	c.	In cell **A14**, type June 5, 2014 and press Enter (note how Excel automatically formats the date).
	d.	In cell **B14** type **=TEXT(A14,"mmmm d, yyyy")**. The second argument of this function is based on specific rules to format numbers and dates. Use the Excel help for that function to know how the formatting works for numbers, date & time, currency, percentages, etc. You will see that the formatting is very intuitive. Sometimes, however, we spend some time developing complex formulas that achieve what simple built-in functions can do more efficiently, as you will now see:
	e.	In cell **C13**, type **=DOLLAR(A13)**.
	f.	In cell **E13**, on your own and using cells **B13** and **B14**, apply a formula that displays On June 5, 2014, sales were $1,250.80. Hint: remember the & symbol?
	g.	Now in cell **E14** write the same formula as the one in **E13** but use cells **A13** and **A14** instead of **B13** and **B14** respectively so that you understand the importance of the **=TEXT( )** function.
	h.	Change the value in cell **A13** to 2540.5 and see what happened to cell **E13**.

STEP **09** Extracting Characters	a.	In cell **A21** type ABCDEFGHI.
	b.	In cell **B21** type **=LEFT(A21,3)**, and in in cell **D21** type **=RIGHT(A21,3)**.
	c.	In cell **C21**, use the **=MID( )** function to extract DEF.

STEP **10** Extracting Characters	a.	In cell **A23**, type Vov is vaking vanana vread (trust me on the spelling for now).
	b.	In cell **C23**, type **=SUBSTITUTE(A23,"v","b")**.
	c.	In cell **E23** type **=REPLACE(C23,1,1,"B")**.
	d.	In cell **H23** type **=SUBSTITUTE(E23,"banana","carrot")**.

STEP **11** Finding and searching within a string		The functions **=FIND( )** and **=SEARCH( )** help us identify the first position of a specific character or string within another string. This example will show you one of the differences between the two functions.
	a.	In cell **A26** type This book is great and Andres looks great in the author photo.
	b.	In cell **A27** type **=FIND("A",A26)**.

c.   In cell **A28** type **=SEARCH("a",A26)**. So what is the difference between **=FIND( )** and **=SEARCH( )**? ☐

Now that you have learned these functions, the following few steps combine some of them to perform specific fancier tasks.

STEP
12
Counting specific characters in a string

a.   In cell **A31**, type **=LEN(E23)-LEN(SUBSTITUTE(E23,"b",""))**. The formula is counting the number of letter *b*s in the string; however, you notice it is case-sensitive so therefore it is not counting the first B. ☐

b.   On your own, in cell **B31**, modify the formula so that it now counts both lower and upper cases (hint: you just need to add in the formula a single function that you already used). If you were unable to do this, consider requesting answer key file via info@excelpro.com. ☐

STEP
13
Dissecting long formulas to understand how they work

Maybe you did not quite understand how the formula in the previous step above is working, so I will show you what to do when you encounter such a problem. Basically, you must *dissect* the formula in parts to see the outputs of each, as follows:

a.   In cell **C31**, type **=SUBSTITUTE(E23,"b","")**, which is part of the formula above (you may copy and paste that part remembering to add the **=** sign at the beginning). The result is Bo is aking anana read. Basically the formula substituted each b with an empty space, which in Excel is represented by "" (two quotation marks one after the other). ☐

b.   In cell **E31**, type **=LEN(SUBSTITUTE(E23,"b",""))**, which is the entire second term of the formula of procedure **a**. The result, 22, is simply the number of characters in Bo is aking anana read, including spaces. ☐

c.   In cell **E32**, type **LEN(E23)**, the first term of our original formula. The result, 26, is the number of characters in Bob is baking banana bread. ☐

d.   In cell **E33**, type **=E32-E31**; the result is identical to what you got in cell **A31**. Now you know how to *dissect* a formula from the inside out to understand how it works. Hooray! ☐

STEP
14
Counting words in a text string

a.   In cell **A34**, type **=(LEN(A26)-LEN(SUBSTITUTE(A26, "great","")))/LEN("great")**. The result indicates the number of times that great is found within cell **A26**. ☐

b.   Why don't you practice *dissecting* the formula above as we did with the previous step? It is important that you exercise this skill so use any empty cells in your sheet to do so. ☐

STEP
15
Extracting the first word from a string and using the IFERROR function

a.   In cells **G2**, **G3** and **G4**, type Elvis Presley, Michael Jackson and Madonna, respectively, and immediately auto-adjust the column width. If you happen to be Madonna, firstly, I am honored that you are reading my book even though I don't like political rants in music shows; secondly, you can pull your name in **G4** from **B2** with the simplest of all formulas. ☐

b.   In cell **H2**, type **=LEFT(G2,FIND(" ",G2)-1)**. This formula says: extract, from cell **G2**, all characters until the first space is found (the **-1** at the end is added so that the space itself is not included). Once more, dissect the formula if you feel like it. ☐

c.   Drag the formula to cells **H3** and **H4**. Oops! It does not work for Madonna! It is because no space is found in the string. Let's solve this with one of my very favorite functions, one that I use all the time. ☐

d.   Change the formula in **H2** to **=IFERROR(LEFT(G2,FIND(" ",G2)-1),G2)**. ☐

e.   Copy the new formula of cell **H2** to overwrite cells **H3** and **H4**. Madonna was fixed! The logic behind **=IFERROR( )** is: *if the result of the first argument is an error, display the second argument, otherwise display the first argument*. In our case, if the string has only one word, simply use that word. Fantastic, huh? From now on you will be using IF statements a lot. Extracting the last word from a string is harder because **=FIND( )** only works from left to right, so we will leave that for another time (find it on the Internet if you ever need to). ☐

16

Typing numbers
as text

Suppose you use codes in the format 001, 002, 003... and you need to keep that format. If you type 001 in any cell Excel treats it as a number, simply displays 1, and your code is lost. Let's see:

a. In cell A36, type 001.

b. In cell B36, type '001 (starting with a single quotation mark, which indicates to Excel to treat whatever follows as text).

c. Drag cell B36 with the mouse to copy it in cells B37 and B38; notice how even if the cells are formatted as text, they are auto-completed in increments.

Your TEXT spreadsheet should look like this (with your own name, of course):

Every time you are doing something, ask yourself: *How can I speed it up with Excel®?*

Part B - Understanding date & time formulas

In this part you will learn how to use specific functions that deal with date and time.

Figure 6. Understanding how dates and time are formatted in Excel is fundamental for making calculations. This part of the book is as important as it gets, and you will see why.

STEP
01
Open and save

a. Open a new Excel file and ☐ save it as **chapter_02_part_B_ date&time_solved.xlsx**.

b. Rename Sheet1 as DATE&TIME. ☐

STEP
02
Date code

a. Type your date of birth in cell **A1** ☐ in this format: *Month Day, Year.*

b. In cell **B1**, recall cell **A1** by using ☐ the formula **=A1** and format it as a number with no decimals and a thousand separator (**Ctrl+1**). That is the number of days between January 1, 1900 and your date of birth.

STEP
03
Exact time

a. Do you know the exact time when you were born? Give your parents a call to find out or simply ☐ invent a time for this step. Type your time of birth in cell **A2** in this format: *hh:mm* (e.g. 21:30) or *hh:mm AM/PM* (e.g. 9:30 PM).

b. Copy the formula of cell **B1** to cell **B2** to know what the numeric format of your time of birth ☐ is. You should get a value between 0 and 1 in cell **B2** (display it with two decimals). Please make sure that you understand what this value represents.

c. In cell **C1**, add the values of cells **B1** and **B2** to get your exact time of birth in days. ☐

STEP
04
Current date and time

a. In cell **A4** type **=TODAY( )**, in cell **B4** type **=NOW( )** and keep the automatic formatting displayed. ☐

b. Recall cell **A4** in cell **A5** and cell **B4** in cell **B5**. ☐

c. Format cell **A5** as a number with 6 decimals and cell **B5** as a number with 12 decimals. Even ☐ though the number displayed in cell **B5** represents current time in fractions of a second, the cell does not change in real time.

d. Type any value in any empty cell and immediately delete it while observing the value in cell **B5**: ☐ you see that the formula is updated only when there is a change in the spreadsheet.

e. Go to the **Formulas** tab and repeatedly press the **Calculate Now** button at the very right while ☐ watching cell **B5**; that is another way to update formula calculations.

Buttons used in this step: Calculate Now

STEP
05
Calculating your exact age

a. In cells **D4** to **I4** type Years, Months, Days, Hours, Minutes and Seconds. ☐

b. In the cells listed in the table below, carefully type (or copy from the eBook if you have it) the ☐ corresponding formulas which will show you the number of years, months, days, hours, minutes and seconds you have lived so far (as you type, notice that when you start using lots of parentheses, Excel helps you with color coding so that you close them properly):

Cell	Formula
D5	=ROUNDDOWN((B5-C1)/365.25,0)
E5	=ROUNDDOWN(((B5-C1)/365.25-D5)*12,0)
F5	=ROUNDDOWN((((B5-C1)/365.25-D5)*12-E5)*30.4375,0)
G5	=ROUNDDOWN(((((B5-C1)/365.25-D5)*12-E5)*30.4375-F5)*24,0)
H5	=ROUNDDOWN((((((B5-C1)/365.25-D5)*12-E5)*30.4375-F5)*24-G5)*60,0)
I5	=((((((B5-C1)/365.25-D5)*12-E5)*30.4375-F5)*24-G5)*60-H5)*60

Don't be overwhelmed by these formulas; this is how they work: cell D5 estimates the number of days elapsed between the current instantaneous time (cell B5) and your birth date (C1) in years. The days are divided by 365.25 to account for leap years, and finally the value is rounded down to zero decimals with =ROUNDDOWN( ).The following cells simply calculate the difference between the value of each previous cell had it not been rounded and the actual rounded value; then the difference is transformed to the units of interest (e.g. × 12 in cell E5 to transform fractions of a year to months). The Seconds cell (I5) does not need to be rounded down.

c. Align all cells in the range D4:I5 to the center, format the Seconds cell (I5) to show two decimals and all others with no decimals. ☐

d. Press the Calculate Now button in the Formulas tab or the F9 key repeatedly to see how seconds and minutes change (especially as seconds approximate to 60). Remember that these results are approximate, given that we are using average days per year (365.25) and days per month (30.4375). ☐

Buttons used in this step: Calculate Now

STEP 06
Introducing names

The formulas above were a bit long, so now we will simplify them by introducing the concepts of names (i.e. applying user-defined labels to cells) and using a simpler function than =ROUNDDOWN( ). But first let's do some calculations that we will need.

a. In cell G1 type =AVERAGE(366,365,365,365) to calculate the average number of days per year including leap years. ☐

b. In cell H1, type =AVERAGE(31,28.25,31,30,31,30,31,31,30,31,30,31) to calculate the average number of days per month. Make sure you understand what both formulas are doing. ☐

c. While in cell G1, go to the Name Box to the left of the Ribbon and type DPY, which stands for days per year (see **Figure 2** to recall the Name Box location if needed). ☐

d. Do the same for cell H1 and label it DPM (days per month). ☐

e. Label cell B5 NOW and cell C1 BIRTH. It is a good idea to label cells with names that remind you what they are, but that are not too long. ☐

f. Notice that you cannot label cells with strings that already refer to a cell reference. For example, in any empty cell, go to the Name Box and type FAB18 to see what happens; go back to the beginning of your worksheet by pressing Ctrl+←. By using names you are complying with recommended **Best Practices** rule #8. ☐

STEP 07
Producing leaner formulas

Refer to **Best Practices** rule #9 about lean formulas while you do this step. We will simplify the formulas of **Step 5** by using =INT( ) instead of =ROUNDDOWN( ), which rounded our numbers using the number of decimals as an argument (set to 0 in **Step 5**). The =INT( ) function rounds down to the lowest integer, so not only does it achieve what we need in one step with fewer arguments but it is also shorter.

a. Before typing these formulas, select rows D5:I5 and copy their formats only to cells D6:I6 (use Paste Special). Now type these formulas in the specified cells: ☐

Cell	Formula
D6	=INT((NOW-BIRTH)/DPY)
E6	=INT(((NOW-BIRTH)/DPY-D6)*12)
F6	=INT((((NOW-BIRTH)/DPY-D6)*12-E6)*DPM)
G6	=INT((((((NOW-BIRTH)/DPY-D6)*12-E6)*DPM-F6)*24)
H6	=INT(((((((NOW-BIRTH)/DPY-D6)*12-E6)*DPM-F6)*24-G6)*60)
I6	=(((((((NOW-BIRTH)/DPY-D6)*12-E6)*DPM-F6)*24-G6)*60-H6)*60

See how these formulas are easier to read and interpret than those of the previous row.

STEP 08
Calculating number of days between dates

a. To calculate the total exact number of days you have lived, in cell A8 simply type the formula ☐
=A5-A1.Since the fundamental unit of time in Excel is one day, the result of that formula gives you the number of days elapsed since your birth and today.

b. The function =NETWORKDAYS( ) estimates the number of days between two dates but excluding ☐
Saturdays, Sundays and holidays (optional and user-defined). Calculate how many working days have taken place since your birth until today in cell B8, assuming no holidays.

The function =DATE( ) merges separate values of year, month and day into a single date.

STEP 09
Merging values into dates

a. In cells A9, B9 and C9 type 2014, 1 and 6, respectively. ☐
b. In cell A10, type the formula =DATE(A9,B9,C9). ☐

The function =WORKDAY( ) provides the date at which a given number of working days expires after a chosen starting date.

STEP 10
Offset dates

a. In cell B10, estimate the date of arrival of a package you sent in the mail on January 6, 2014 ☐
(which you got from the previous step in cell A10), if the post office assures you that it will take 15 working days for them to deliver it and there are no upcoming holidays.

b. Format cell B10 to be shown as a date in the format *yyyy-mm-dd*. ☐

STEP 11
Retrieving years, months, days and weekdays

a. In cell A12, type =YEAR(A1). ☐
b. In cell B12 type =MONTH(A1). ☐
c. In cell C12 type =DAY(A1), and in cell D12, type =WEEKDAY(A1). Understand what these formulas ☐
are providing.
d. In cell E12, use the =TEXT( ) function to display the week day on which you were born (for ☐
example, Wednesday).

STEP 12
Displaying time

a. To display current time, in cell A14 type the formula =NOW( )-TODAY( ) and format the cell in ☐
hh:mm:ss.
b. To display any time, in cell B14 type =TIME(9,80,15) and notice what Excel does with the 80 minutes. ☐

STEP 13
Retrieving hours, minutes and seconds

a. In cell A15, type =HOUR(B5). ☐
b. In cell B15, type =MINUTE(B5). ☐
c. In cell C15, type =SECOND(B5). ☐
d. You are done with **Part B**! Have fun by pressing F9 or the Calculate Now button repeatedly as ☐
if your life depended on how fast you do it.

Buttons used in this step: Calculate Now 🖩

Your DATE&TIME spreadsheet should look like the image below, with your own numbers; close and save your file after checking:

	A	B	C	D	E	F	G	H	I	J
1	30-Sep-78	28,763	28,763.88				365.25	30.4375		
2	21:00	0.88								
3										
4	09/07/2015	09/07/2015 02:46		Years	Months	Days	Hours	Minutes	Seconds	
5	42194.000000	42194.115806597200		36	9	7	7	16	45.69	
6				36	9	7	7	16	45.69	
7										
8	13,431	9594								
9	2014	1	6							
10	06-Jan-14	2014-01-27								
11										
12	1978	9	30	7 Saturday						
13										
14	02:46:46	10:20 AM								
15	2	46	46							
16										
17										

Figure 7. Organic Chemistry professor or Excel genius?

Part C - Understanding logical formulas

Logical statements are fundamental in Excel. While you have already applied some and will continue to use them throughout the book, it is impossible not to include this small section paying educational tribute to such a crucial programming skill.

Before you begin this part, go to the Formulas tab and glimpse the formulas in the Logical button (if you place the cursor over each formula, a box appears with a brief explanation).

STEP

01

Open, save and analyze

a. Open the file **chapter_02_part_C_grades.xlsx**.

b. Analyze your database. As you can tell, you are the Organic Chemistry professor (**Figure 7**) at the end of the term; you must calculate final grades and this task will demonstrate that sometimes we don't have any choice other than using logical functions. This is because passing a course is commonly subject to a few restrictions. Cells **H2**, **I2** and **J2** indicate the percentages that the lab assignments, midterm and final exam contribute to the final grade. All grades are over 100 points. To pass the course, a student must:

• score more than or equal to 50 points in the weighted average of labs, midterm and final exam;

• have no missing labs; and

• show lecture attendance of at least 50% **or** lab attendance of at least 80%. In the next steps, we will include these rules to calculate an Official grade, Rank and Standing.

STEP
02
Calculate raw grade

a. In cell **K5**, type a formula that will multiply the Labs, Midterm and Exam grades for each student by their weight on their final grades in cells **H2**, **I2** and **J2** respectively.

b. Propagate the formula that you just typed to cells **K6:K133**; I hope you remembered to correctly set up fixed references in the **K5** formula for it to work downward; if not, don't worry; it still happens to me every now and then.

STEP
03
Calculating official grade and dissecting a formula again

The official grade must simply show the same as the raw grade if the student got an overall raw grade of less than 50, but must be reduced to 49 if the student got a higher raw grade but does not comply with all the requirements of procedure **1b** above. We will now work this out by building a beautiful logical statement.

a. Before we type the formula we need, it would be a good idea to independently check that it works. For this we will add some color aids with *conditional formatting* rules which highlight our restrictions. Make records in column E appear with the built-in Light Red Fill with Dark Red Text option if Lecture attendance [%] is lower than 50%. Use the same color to highlight Lab attendance [%] lower than 80%, one or more Missing labs, Raw grade and Official grade lower than 50 and Standing equal to the letter F (do it even though these last two columns have no values yet). Once you finish with the conditional formatting, manually scroll through the records to observe if there are students with a raw grade higher than 50 whose lecture or lab attendance or missing labs will make them fail the course. We are now ready to use a formula that works automatically.

b. In cell **L5**, type the formula **=IF(K5<50,K5,IF(AND(G5=0,OR(E5>=50,F5>=80)),K5,49))**. This formula is saying: *Why bother if the raw grade is below 50; just retrieve it (if* **K5<50**, *just use* **K5**). *If this first test is false, which means the grade is 50 or more, then evaluate if there are no missing labs* **(G5=0)** *and if either the lecture attendance is higher than 50% or the lab attendance is higher than 80%* **(OR(E5>=50,F5>=80))**. *If this second test works, the student will pass with the raw grade untouched* **(K5)**, *but if not, it will be forced to become 49.* If you are an Excel® 2016 user and Office® 365 subscriber, feel free to modify the formula using the **=IFS( )** function instead.

c. If the explanation given above was not enough for you to see the logic of this formula, you may want to dissect it into pieces to fully understand it. For example, type the **=AND(G5=0,OR(E5>=50,F5>=80))** part of it in cell **O5** and temporarily propagate it a few cells down to see what the outcome is. You can do the same with the **=OR(E5>=50,F5>=80)** part in cells **P5** and below. When you are done, clear the **O** and **P** columns. Remember that this procedure is what I call *dissecting a formula piece by piece* and you have done it already.

d. Propagate the formula in cell **L5** to the cells below, make sure that it is working properly and analyze it in depth. It is extremely important that you understand every single piece of it and its functioning as a whole. Answer this question yourself: how many students with a raw grade higher than 50 failed the course due to other reasons?

e. When analyzing your grades, notice that the student with the highest Official grade got a 100.7. This is because you are a professor who offers generous bonus points, but the university grading system does not accept grades exceeding 100. On your own, modify the formula in column **L** so that if you get a grade higher than 100, it changes it to 100. Hint: there are several ways to do it but one of the simplest involves adding a single function outside the first and primary **=IF( )** statement. If you are struggling to achieve this, check the corresponding answer key file that you can request as explained in the **Download working files and answer keys** section.

STEP
04
Final touches

a. Use **=RANK( )** in the Rank column to show a ranking of students where 1 is assigned to the highest grade, 2 to the second highest, and so on. Use the help, if necessary, to understand that function.

b. Apply a conditional formatting rule to the Rank column so that your top ten students are highlighted with a Green Fill with Dark Green Text pattern.

c. For Standing, create a formula (indeed much shorter than the one in procedure **3b**) that results in a P if the Official grade is higher or equal to 50, or else displays an F.

Figure 8. There are no losers at intersections in your city, so traffic lights are always green —the color of Excel.

Part D - Apply your knowledge to a typical example

In the following example, you are a City of Vancouver municipality supervisor in charge of three crews that were hired in 2013 to install traffic lights like the ones shown in **Figure 8**.

The crews worked on random days given their availability to go out to the field but their only mandate was to install all the traffic lights between April 1 and September 30. The job was finished and they sent you the file **chapter_02_Part_D_installation_hours.xlsx** with their working hours for you to process their payments.

In the next steps, you will be applying text, *date & time* and *logical* functions you learned in **Part A**, **Part B**, and **Part C**, and you will reinforce the use of names.

STEP
01
Open, save and organize

a.   Open the file **chapter_02_Part_D_installation_hours.xlsx**, and immediately save it with the name **chapter_02_Part_D_installation_hours_solved.xlsx**. After you explore the file you immediately notice that the crews included separate sheets for their dates and working hours. According to *Best Practices* rule #6, centralize databases with equivalent information to favor functionality (for example, to type formulas only once!).   ☐

b.   In the CREW 1 sheet, add a column to the left of the Date, label it Crew in the table header and fill the column data with the number 1 all the way down (just repeat the 1).   ☐

c.   Copy and paste the data from the CREW 2 and CREW 3 sheets in the CREW 1 sheet below the data of crew 1 and in the first column make sure you identify records from crew 2 and crew 3.   ☐

d.   Delete the CREW 2 and CREW 3 sheets and rename the CREW 1 sheet as WORK HOURS; also delete the contents of cell **B2** and in cell **A2** type Work hours; move the contents of cells **B3** and **B4** one position to the left.   ☐

STEP
02
Creating proper dates

Your crews were not considering good practices of Excel and they typed the dates of the second column as text. To avoid issues (e.g. sorting records by date would eliminate the chronological order), we need to write proper dates from the text.

a.   Insert a column after the Date column and label it Month (text).   ☐

b.   In the column you just created, use **=LEFT( )** to extract the three letters of the month from the records in the Date column.   ☐

c.   Add another column after the Month (text) column, label it Month (#).   ☐

d.   Select the Month (#) column and format the cells as numbers with no decimals (Ctrl+1).   ☐

e.   In cell **D7**, type the formula **=MONTH(C7&1)** and drag it down to fill all records in the column; notice what that formula did (this is a mystery formula whose syntax explanation is not found in textbooks or the Excel help).   ☐

f.   Add another column after the Month (#) column and label it Day (#); fill it down starting on the **E7** cell with the formula **=RIGHT(B7,2)**.   ☐

g.   Rename cell **B6** to Date (text) and add another column after Day (#) labeled Date (#).   ☐

h.   Based on the columns you have so far and knowing that all records belong to the year 2013, use **=DATE( )** in the new Date (#) column to fill in its records and format them in the *yyyy-mm-dd* style; compare your results in that column with the original Date (text) records to make sure it worked consistently for all.   ☐

<table>
<tr><td>

STEP
03
Working lean

</td><td>

We followed all the procedures of the previous step in separate columns for educational purposes so that you see what each formula does separately; now we will try a leaner approach to follow our ***Best Practices*** rule #9 about being lean (one formula does it all!).

</td></tr>
</table>

a. Add another column after the Date (#) column, format all of it *yyyy-mm-dd* and label it Date in the header. ☐

b. In one single formula line starting on cell G7, do everything you did in separate columns in the previous step to generate numeric dates again. In other words, how would you get a proper formatted date without creating intermediate columns? (hint: functions can have other functions inside). Now that you have a proper date in the Date column obtained from a single lean formula, we don't need the previous columns; however, you don't want to delete them for educational purposes to remind you of this exercise. ☐

c. To enjoy the best of two worlds, select the columns from Date (text) to Date (#), Right Click on any location of their column letters, and select Hide. Hiding cells is sometimes very useful to avoid displaying internal calculations. Notice that the column letters now skip from A to G. You can unhide the columns by selecting the visible columns next to the hidden ones and pressing Right Click + Unhide; try this if you wish but leave columns B to F hidden in your final file. ☐

STEP
04
Formatting

a. Apply auto-width to all visible columns, center your range's cells, apply some color to your header row, add borders and hide the gridlines (optional). ☐

b. If your hidden columns re-appeared when adjusting the column widths, hide them again. ☐

c. Keep your title rows (cells A2:A4) aligned to the left and make cell A2 bold and font size 16. ☐

d. Freeze panes so that rows 1 to 6 are always visible. ☐

STEP
05
Calculating
daily pay

a. Add five columns after the Lunch [min] column and label them Weekday, Total hours, Regular hours, Overtime hours and Payment [$]. ☐

b. Format the Weekday column as numbers with no decimals and the other four new columns as numbers with two decimals. ☐

c. In cell L2 write Regular hours:, in cell L3 write $/regular hour: and in cell L4 write $/overtime hour:; type 7.5, 18 and 25 in cells M2, M3 and M4, respectively. ☐

d. Use the Name box to label cell M2 as RH, cell M3 as PRH and cell M4 as POH, *which stand for regular hours, pay for regular hours and pay for overtime hours respectively.* ☐

e. In cells K7:K77, use **=WEEKDAY( )** to obtain the day of the week of each record and make sure you use the option to start the week on Monday (i.e. Monday = 1; Tuesday = 2, ... Sunday = 7). ☐

f. In the Total hours column, calculate the total number of hours worked by the crews each day (hint: you need a simple formula that uses the Time start, Time end and Lunch [min] columns; remember how Excel codes time to solve this). Your formula should produce 7.5 in cell L7 and 9.5 in cell L9. Now we need to understand the **=IF( )** function to calculate regular and overtime hours. As specified in the sheet, overtime is any work beyond 7.5 hours during a weekday and any hour worked during Saturdays and Sundays. ☐

g. In cell M7, type the formula **=IF(K7>5,0,IF(L7<=RH,L7,IF(L7>RH,RH,0)))** and copy it down to all cells in the column. Take your time to understand what the formula does and the logic behind. As always, Office® 365 users may apply the **=IFS( )** function instead. ☐

h. In cell N7, type the formula **=L7-M7** and copy it down to all cells in the column. Now check if both formulas work correctly by remembering what overtime is and making sure that the sum of columns M and N is equal to the Total hours calculated in column L. ☐

i. In the Payment [$] column, calculate the salary per day per person considering that each crew has two members (the Payment [$] column should reflect the individual payment for each crew member assuming that both worked equally for the hours reported). The first value you get in cell O7 should be 187.50. ☐

STEP
06
Calculating
total pay

a. In cells O2, O3 and O4, type CREW 1, CREW 2 and CREW 3, respectively. Now you will learn the useful =SUMIF( ) function to calculate the total payment for each member of the crews.
b. Format cells P2:Q4 as numbers with two decimals with a thousand separator.
c. In cell P2, type the formula =SUMIF($A$7:$A$77,RIGHT(O2,1),$O$7:$O$77); then copy it to cells P3 and P4 and understand what it does (this formula is in the **Select formula index** at the end).
d. Type $/person in cell P1 and make it **bold**.

STEP
07
Evaluating crews

a. You are wondering which crew was more efficient so in cell Q1 type $/light and make it **bold**.
b. In cell Q2, use the value in cell P2 and another =SUMIF( ) statement to estimate the **total** cost per light (remember that the value in cell P2 represents the payment to a single crew member and all crews have two people).
c. Copy your formula of the previous procedure to cells Q3 and Q4.
d. In cell S2, calculate the total labor cost of your operation.
e. In cell S3, estimate what that total cost would have been if all three crews were as efficient as the most efficient crew, and calculate the money you would have saved in cell S4.
f. Format cells S2, S3 and S4 as numbers with two decimals and a thousand separator.

That's it! The upper part of your WORK HOURS spreadsheet should look like this (with your own color):

	A	G	H	I	J	K	L	M	N	O	P	Q	R	S	T
1											$/person	$/light			
2	**Work hours**						Regular hours:	7.50		CREW 1	3,907.25	101.49		21,612.00	
3	2013						$/regular hour:	18.00		CREW 2	3,618.75	100.52		20,934.12	
4	Overtime: weekends and weekdays past 7.5 hours						$/overtime hour:	25.00		CREW 3	3,280.00	96.47		677.88	
5															
6	Crew	Date	Time start	Time end	Lunch [min]	Weekday	Total hours	Regular hours	Overtime hours	Payment [$]	Lights installed				
7	1	2013-04-07	8:00 AM	4:00 PM	30	7	7.50	0.00	7.50	187.50	3				
8	1	2013-04-09	8:00 AM	4:00 PM	30	2	7.50	7.50	0.00	135.00	3				
9	1	2013-04-10	8:00 AM	6:00 PM	30	3	9.50	7.50	2.00	185.00	3				
10	1	2013-04-11	8:00 AM	5:30 PM	30	4	9.00	7.50	1.50	172.50	4				
11	1	2013-04-20	10:00 AM	4:00 PM	30	6	5.50	0.00	5.50	137.50	2				
12	1	2013-04-26	8:00 AM	4:00 PM	30	5	7.50	7.50	0.00	135.00	3				
13	1	2013-05-04	8:00 AM	4:00 PM	30	6	7.50	0.00	7.50	187.50	3				
14	1	2013-05-11	8:00 AM	4:00 PM	45	6	7.25	0.00	7.25	181.25	3				
15	1	2013-05-21	8:00 AM	4:00 PM	30	2	7.50	7.50	0.00	135.00	3				
16	1	2013-05-25	8:00 AM	4:00 PM	30	6	7.50	0.00	7.50	187.50	3				
17	1	2013-06-16	8:00 AM	4:00 PM	30	7	7.50	0.00	7.50	187.50	2				
18	1	2013-06-18	8:30 AM	6:00 PM	30	2	9.00	7.50	1.50	172.50	5				
19	1	2013-07-06	8:00 AM	4:00 PM	30	6	7.50	0.00	7.50	187.50	3				
20	1	2013-07-11	8:00 AM	4:00 PM	60	4	7.00	7.00	0.00	126.00	3				
21	1	2013-07-14	8:00 AM	4:00 PM	30	7	7.50	0.00	7.50	187.50	4				
22	1	2013-07-16	9:00 AM	3:00 PM	30	2	5.50	5.50	0.00	99.00	3				
23	1	2013-07-18	8:00 AM	4:00 PM	30	4	7.50	7.50	0.00	135.00	3				
24	1	2013-07-20	8:00 AM	4:00 PM	30	6	7.50	0.00	7.50	187.50	3				
25	1	2013-07-26	8:00 AM	4:00 PM	30	5	7.50	7.50	0.00	135.00	2				
26	1	2013-08-05	8:00 AM	4:00 PM	45	1	7.25	7.25	0.00	130.50					

5. Review of functions used

=AVERAGE( )	=IF( )	=NOW( )	=TEXT( )
=CHAR( )	=IFERROR( )	=PROPER( )	=TIME( )
=CODE( )	=INT( )	=REPLACE( )	=TODAY( )
=CONCATENATE( )	=LEFT( )	=REPT( )	=TRIM( )
=DATE( )	=LEN( )	=RIGHT( )	=UPPER( )
=DAY( )	=LOWER( )	=ROUNDDOWN( )	=WEEKDAY( )
=DOLLAR( )	=MID( )	=SEARCH( )	=WORKDAY( )
=EXACT( )	=MINUTE( )	=SECOND( )	=YEAR( )
=FIND( )	=MONT( )	=SUBSTITUTE( )	
=HOUR( )	=NETWORKDAYS( )	=SUMIF( )	

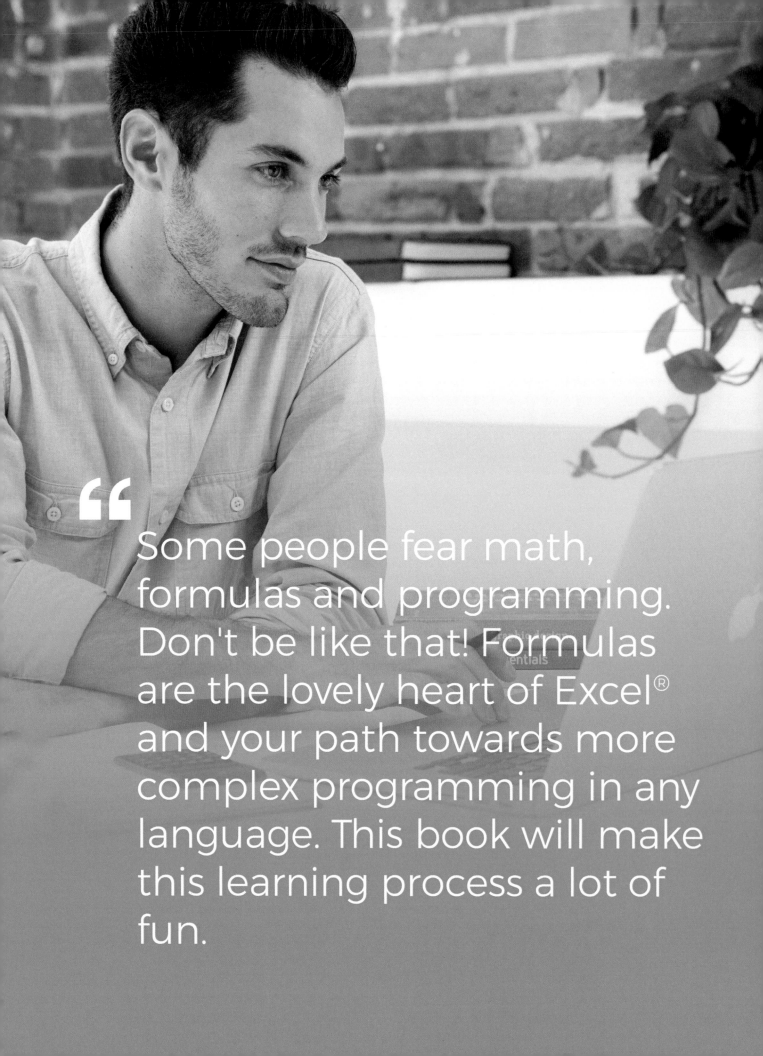

"Some people fear math, formulas and programming. Don't be like that! Formulas are the lovely heart of Excel® and your path towards more complex programming in any language. This book will make this learning process a lot of fun.

CHAPTER 3

Math formulas

1. Introduction and learning objectives

In this chapter you will learn more useful Excel functions with emphasis on those in the *math & trigonometry* category, as well as reinforce the use of names. In **Part A** you will be performing basic count and sum operations. In **Part B** you will work with some very simple formulas that will celebrate your golden algebra days at school. In **Part C**, you will apply formulas that count and sum in a very practical example. This chapter also focuses on the use of names to make formulas easier to visualize, and a few additional tricks. Remember that as you follow the instructions of this chapter and achieve its learning objectives, you are becoming a real Excel programmer.

The learning objectives are:

1. Reinforce the use of *names*.
2. Understand the use of formulas that count and sum.
3. Understand how to write an algebraic formula in Excel.
4. Use *hyperlinks* and images to make your files more professional.
5. Reinforce the use of *IF* statements for formula consistency.

2. Specific skills

1. **Creating simple formulas that count and sum:** counting cells by their contents; counting cells that meet specific criteria; performing cumulative sums; performing conditional summing and counting.
2. **Creating and managing *names*** based on cell arrays, formulas and nonexistent locations.
3. **Transforming common algebraic notation to Excel language:** using sphere volume equations to learn how Excel treats algebraic expressions.
4. **Inserting images:** making your spreadsheets stand out with colorful images.
5. **Reinforcing your knowledge of logical formulas:** using proper *IF* statements with multiple criteria to produce a single consolidated outcome.
6. **Using *hyperlinks*** as formatted buttons to navigate through a workbook.

7. **Indenting cell contents** for enhanced display.
8. **Displaying today's date** with the Ctrl+; shortcut.
9. **Hiding and unhiding column and row headings** to make people believe that our spreadsheet is not Excel.

3. Background

3.1 Using names for arrays, formulas and nonexistent locations

In the previous chapter you practiced applying names to individual cells. Now you will learn to use names for cell arrays and pre-defined formulas based or not on specific locations within your workbook. It is also possible to store other values as names without them being in a specific cell. To do all this you just need to Click the Define Name button in the Formulas tab.

3.2 Quick review of how math is performed in Excel

Recall from **Table 1** (**Chapter 2**) that Excel handles mathematical operations exactly the same way as in common algebra. One skill that you will reinforce in this chapter is translating to Excel's language a regular mathematical formula that you may encounter elsewhere.

For example, the formula used to solve for x in a standard quadratic equation written as $ax^2 + bx + c = 0$ is:

$$x = \frac{-b \pm \sqrt{b^2 - 4ac}}{2a}$$

To enter this formula in Excel, one must be aware of the order in which the operations are made (**Table 1**) so that parentheses are in the right place. The correct way of writing one of the solutions for this equation in Excel if a is stored in cell A1, b in B1 and c in C1, would therefore be:

=(-B1+(B1^2-4*A1*C1)^0.5)/(2*A1)

If you took some time to label cell A1 as a, B1 as b and C1 as c, typing the following formula in Excel will work too:

=(-b+(b^2-4*a*c)^0.5)/(2*a)

Notice how our **Best Practices** rules #8 and #9 are applied by labelling our cells to produce the formula above. You will exercise the extremely important skill of writing algebraic equations in Excel with simple examples in this chapter.

ProTip

Remember the most important Excel® rule: always link your spreadsheet cells through referenced formulas and never type the same content twice. That way, if you update one cell, everything else will magically change.

4. Procedures

Through the following steps, you will complete all tasks described in **Section 2**, but not necessarily in the same order. Remember our legend convention as you read: **file name**, Excel location (tab, menu, button, dialog box, control, option or cell coordinates), keyboard or mouse button(s), **formula**, typed data and procedure.

Part A uses simple exercises to teach you the use of specific functions and formulas, while in **Part B** and **Part C** you will directly apply part of this knowledge to typical, extremely cool examples.

Figure 9. What is the value of red or white cars in this lot? If you have a proper database, Excel can tell you in a second.

Part A - Simple counting and summing

STEP
01
Open and save

a. Open file **chapter_03_part_A_count_and_sum.xlsx** and save it in a safe location of your hard drive as **chapter_03_part_A_count_and_sum_solved.xlsx**. Remember to constantly save the file with **Ctrl+S** as you make progress. ☐

b. Make sure that you are in the BASIC COUNTING sheet for the following steps. ☐

STEP
02
Counting total, blank and filled cells

a. Before starting with all the exercises in **Part A**, we need to label our data, so select cells B4:C18 and then type CELLS in the Name Box (see **Figure 2** in **Chapter 1** to remember where it is). ☐

b. In cell E4 type **=ROWS(CELLS)*COLUMNS(CELLS)**; those functions count the number of rows and columns, respectively, so combined they are used to count the total number of cells. ☐

c. In cell E5, type the formula **=COUNTBLANK(CELLS)**. ☐

d. In cell E6, type **=COUNTA(CELLS)**. Manually verify if this formula is working correctly. ☐

STEP
03
Counting numeric, logical, error and text cells

a. In cell E7, type **=COUNT(CELLS)**. The **=COUNT( )** function is the simplest of all and is used to count numbers only. ☐

b. There are only two logical outputs in Excel: TRUE or FALSE. This means that if you type them in a cell, Excel does not recognize them as text unless you include the single quotation mark at the beginning ('TRUE). So, to count the total number of logical outputs, in cell E8 type **=COUNTIF(CELLS,TRUE)+COUNTIF(CELLS,FALSE)**. The **=COUNTIF( )** function is used for conditional counting and has two arguments. Make sure you understand, through this example, how it works. ☐

c. Another possible output in Excel, after typing a formula, is an **error**. To learn more about that, type excel formula errors in your favorite online search engine. You should find #####, #DIV/0!, #N/A, #NAME?, #VALUE!, and others. Typing those errors in Excel's help (F1) leads to a detailed explanation of their causes and how to deal with each, but this book will teach you too. ☐

d. Counting all errors at once in a range of cells requires the use of *array formulas*, which are outside the scope of this book, so for now we will just count the number of #NAME? errors in our CELLS, by typing in cell E9 the formula **=COUNTIF(CELLS,"#NAME?")**. By the way, the #NAME? error occurs when a formula uses a name that has not been defined by the user; go to cell B18 and look at the formula there to understand what I mean. ☐

e. Unfortunately, Excel does not have a function equivalent to **=COUNT( )** that could be used to count text strings in a range, and doing this directly also requires more complex array formulas. So for now we will count text cells by subtracting the numerical, logical, error and blank cells from our CELLS range. To do so, in cell E10 type **=E4-E5-E7-E8-E9**, and verify that it works (remember that TRUE and FALSE are not text). ☐

STEP

04

Counting cells
that meet
specific criteria

a.   In cell E11, use =COUNTIF( ) to count the number of cells containing the value 15 in the CELLS range. You are on your own now!   ☐

b.   In cell E12, type =COUNTIF(CELLS,">4").   ☐

c.   Fill the proper formula for cell E13.   ☐

d.   In cell E14, type =COUNTIF(CELLS,"T**") to determine how many cells contain text that starts with the letter "T").   ☐

e.   Type the proper formulas for cells E15 and E16. Notice that =COUNTIF( ) is not case-sensitive.   ☐

f.   In cell E17, type =COUNTIF(CELLS,"???").   ☐

g.   Type the proper formula for cell E18. You now intuitively understand the logic of using * and ? in the second argument of =COUNTIF( ), but if you want to officially learn more, Click on the function's help.   ☐

h.   Knowing that the * symbol is used to identify text, can you think of a formula for cell E19 that will directly count the number of cells containing text?   ☐

i.   In cell E20, type =COUNTIF(CELLS,">"&B13).   ☐

j.   In cell E21, type the proper formula.   ☐

STEP

05

Counting cells
that meet
multiple
criteria

a.   In cell E22 type =COUNTIFS(CELLS,">2",CELLS,"<15").   ☐

b.   Type the proper formula in cell E23.   ☐

c.   In cell E24 type =COUNTIF(CELLS,"Use")+COUNTIF(CELLS,"that").   ☐

d.   Create the proper formula for cell E25.   ☐

Your BASIC COUNTING sheet should have the following values:

	A	B	C	D	E	F
1						
2		**Fun counting exercise**				
3						
4		Use	s		30	Total number of cells
5		1	in		3	Number of blank cells
6		exercise	Excel		27	Number of filled cells
7		2	&		7	Numeric values
8		understand			2	Logical outputs
9		how			1	#NAME? errors
10		TRUE	that		17	Text cells (*non-elegant, non-robust and questionable way*)
11		it	17		2	Cells with #15
12		is	15		3	Cells >4
13		4	FALSE		3	Cells <3
14		U	that		2	Cells that start with "T"
15		2	Excel		3	Cells that end with "t"
16		work	15		4	Cells that contain "a"
17		with	hard		2	Cells with exactly three characters
18		#NAME?			5	Cells with exactly four characters
19					17	Text cells (*elegant way*)
20					4	Cells > cell B13
21					4	Cells < cell B7
22					1	Cells >2 and <15
23					3	Cells >=1 and <4
24					3	Cells with "Use" or "that"
25					4	Cells with "work" or >4
26						

STEP
06
Cumulative
sum

a. Go to the BASIC SUMMING sheet and in cell C17 type =SUM(C5:C16).

b. In cell D5 type =SUM(C$5:C5).

c. Drag the formula down until you reach cell D16. Note how the semi-relative reference setup helps you obtain the cumulative sum.

d. Update the table by filling cells C13:C16 with the following values, in this order from September to December: 1120, 650, 680, and 2350.

Your BASIC SUMMING sheet should look like this:

	A	B	C	D	E	F
1						
2		**Money spent on parties by month** (2014)				
3						
4		**Month**	**Amount [$]**	**Accumulated**		
5		January	200	200		
6		February	525	725		
7		March	800	1,525		
8		April	2,510	4,035		
9		May	600	4,635		
10		June	2,500	7,135		
11		July	1,500	8,635		
12		August	300	8,935		
13		September	1,120	10,055		
14		October	650	10,705		
15		November	680	11,385		
16		December	2,350	13,735		
17		TOTAL	13,735	-		
18						
19						

The following steps correspond to conditional summing using a single criterion (=SUMIF( ) function) and multiple criteria (=SUMIFS( ) function). These are equivalent to the counting functions =COUNTIF( ) and COUNTIFS( ) which you have already used, so this will be done in the blink of an eye but using a typical example. You are the store manager of a retail store and the CONDITIONAL SUMMING sheet includes all the sales, by invoice #, that you have had so far in your business. We will now use some simple formulas to get very interesting information about your sales, which just represent examples of what you can do.

STEP
07
Sales by
employee, date
and method

a. In cell J5 of the CONDITIONAL SUMMING sheet, type =SUMIF(and select cells H5:H1555 to fill the range argument (use Ctrl+Shift+↓), then type "Martin" as the second argument, and finally select cells G5:G1555 as the third argument in the function. So it should be =SUMIF(H5:H1555,"Martin",G5:G1555) (this formula is in the **Select formula index** at the end).

b. Before filling the next formulas and thinking of how laborious it would be to select cells with the mouse every time, let's apply some names. Select cells B5:B1555 and label them as INVOICE in the Name Box and do the same for the corresponding cells applying the names DATE, METHOD, AMOUNT, TAX, TOTAL and SOLDBY. It takes a little while but you will only do it once!

c. In cell J6, type =SUMIF(SOLDBY,"<>Maria",TOTAL). Do you realize that in this case it is easier and more elegant to work with names rather than cell numbers as in procedure a above?

d. In cell J7, type =SUMIF(DATE,">"&(DATE(2012,12,31)),TOTAL). Make sure you understand exactly what all these formulas are doing! You need to follow their logic.

e. Type the proper formula in cell J8.

STEP
08
Sales by employee, date and method

a. Insert a column between Date and Method, type Year in the header (cell D4), and a formula in cell D5 that extracts the year from cell C5 (we used this function before but you can exercise your ability to find it from scratch). You may need to format cell D5 as a number with no decimals. Finally, propagate the formula and formatting to cells D6:D1555. ☐

b. Label cells D5:D1555 as YEAR and hide this new column D as we only need it for internal calculations. ☐

c. Count the number of invoices generated in 2012 and 2013 in cells K10 and K11 respectively. ☐

d. Write a proper formula for cell K12. ☐

In the steps above you were only required to write simple =SUMIF( ) or =COUNTIF( ) statements. Now we will spice it up a little. I will show you the first example and you will complete the next two on your own.

STEP
09
Sales by employee, date and method

a. In cell K14, type =COUNTIF(METHOD,"Debit")/COUNT(TOTAL)*100 and dissect it if required to understand what it's doing (remember: **Step 13** from **Part A**, **Chapter 2**). ☐

b. Write a proper formula for cell K15. ☐

c. If commissions for employees are 3.5% of their sales **before tax**, type a formula in cell K16 using =SUMIFS( ) that will calculate Ryan's commissions for 2013. ☐

d. Now type a formula in cell K17 that complies with the three criteria required by cell L17. Do you realize how easy it is to type these formulas if you have the data properly labeled? ☐

The upper part of your CONDITIONAL SUMMING sheet should be:

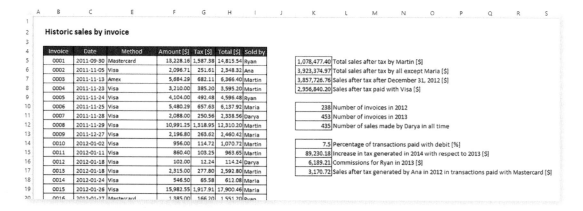

We are ready to move on to **Part B!** Good job!

Part B - Cool mathematical formulas

It is very important that you understand how to translate the algebraic language of an equation that you find in a textbook or the Internet into a mathematical formula that Excel can understand. Such is the purpose of this **Part B**, which is not a hard task at all. Refer to **Table 1** (**Chapter 2**) where a list of the mathematical operators and the order in which they are internally processed by Excel are shown.

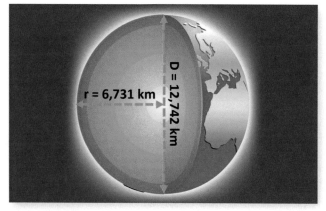

Figure 10. Earth's diameter (*D*) and radius (*r*).

The beautiful Earth where you live is a spheroid whose average diameter (*D*) is 12,742 km (7,918 mi), as shown in **Figure 10**.

The average radius (r) is therefore 6,371 km (3,959 mi). If you took all the water on the planet and made a sphere out of it, how would its diameter compare to the Earth's? All you need to know for **Part B** are the formulas to calculate volume (V) and area (A) of a sphere:

Equation 1:

Equation 2:

$$V = \frac{4}{3}\pi r^3$$

$$A = 4\pi r^2$$

As you remember very well from school, π (pi) is a constant equivalent to 3.14159, which represents the number of diameters that fit in its corresponding circumference. In the first exercise of this section we will be given volumes of water in order to calculate the diameter of the sphere that would contain them. Solving for r in both equations above, we get:

Equation 3:

Equation 4:

$$r = \sqrt[3]{\frac{3V}{4\pi}}$$

$$r = \sqrt{\frac{A}{4\pi}}$$

To calculate the diameters of spheres, we simply multiply the radius by 2:

Equation 5:

Equation 6:

$$D = 2 \times \sqrt[3]{\frac{3V}{4\pi}}$$

$$D = 2 \times \sqrt{\frac{A}{4\pi}}$$

Now we are ready to begin this exercise!

STEP
01
Open, save and format

a. Open the file **chapter_03_part_B_cool_calculations.xlsx** and save it in a safe location as **chapter_03_part_B_cool_calculations_solved.xlsx**. There is an Imperial unit version called **chapter_03_part_B_cool_calculations_imperial.xlsx**; choose your preference, but remember that the metric system is science's golden standard.

b. Look at the table in the sheet WATER RESOURCES: it shows the volume of water present on Earth; it is divided into saline and freshwater, and the latter is further classified into ice & glaciers, groundwater, etc. Notice the beautiful graphs to the right which show the data visually and start to get excited because you will learn how to create them in **Chapter 5.** The volumes in the table are in km³ or mi³ but the numbers are so large that you cannot possibly visualize what they represent; hence, we had to use scientific notation. The total amount of water (cell C13) is 1.384 billion km³, which is 1,384,000,000 (332 million mi³).

c. Note that the total in cell C13 is simply adding cells C5 and C6. Let's use indentation to help visualize the table a bit better. Select cells B7:B12 → Ctrl+1 → Alignment, and type 2 in the Indent box.

d. Make the font size 10 in cells B7:F12. Now the table clearly shows how freshwater is subdivided into categories.

STEP
02
Calculations

a. Fill cells E7:E12, with a formula that calculates the percentage each category represents with respect to the freshwater volume (column D shows the percentage with respect to the total). ☐

b. We will use the **=PI( )** function in the formulas below so let's show you how it works: in cell G2, type **=PI( )** and see what you get as a result. This function, as you can see, has no arguments because it is just a constant with a lot of decimals. Each year as computers get more powerful, scientists try to come up with a more precise value of π, which nowadays has more than 13 trillion digits identified (who needs that kind of precision?). Excel's built-in value is rather humble, with only 14 decimal places (check this if you wish). ☐

c. Delete the contents of cell G2 as we only needed it for educational purposes. ☐

d. Select cells C5:C13 and label them as V in the Name Box. ☐

e. In cell F5, type **=2*(3*V/(4*PI()))^(1/3)**. Now it is important that you see how this formula is identical to **Equation 5** above. Compare them and see how the parentheses are used based on the precedence order of the operations (**Table 1**, **Chapter 2**). For example, we need to put the **1/3** at the end in parentheses so that Excel does the division before the exponentiation. This is basic algebra. ☐

f. Copy the formula of cell F5 to cells F6:F13 but do not drag it with the mouse because that will change our cell formats and table border. Use Ctrl+C and the Paste Formulas command instead. ☐

You have worked incredibly hard so far. Maybe it's time to take a short break, brew some coffee, go cycling or watch YouTube epic fail compilations. Perhaps you can call a friend you have not seen in years, buy mother's day gifts online for mommy for the next five years in advance, or read Thea Beckman's hilarious and educational blog *Why? Because Science*.

STEP
03
Storing names without cells and making formulas cleaner

a. Go to Formulas → Name Manager → New... then type PI in the Name Box and **=PI( )** in the Refers to box, then Click OK. Finally, close the Name Manager dialog box, where you should now see both PI and V. Do you somehow dislike the many parentheses that our formula of cells F5:F13 include? We can get rid of a couple as an excuse to show you how to create names without the need for referring them to a cell or group of cells, like we did with V. This is particularly easy when storing constants so we will create our own π name. ☐

b. Go to cell F5 and manually delete the ( ) after **PI** so that it now looks **=2*(3*V/(4*PI))^(1/3)**. That is a bit leaner than the previous version but, most importantly, you learned how to store a name without cells. ☐

c. Copy the formula down to cells F6:F13 again using the Paste Formulas command. ☐

Buttons used in this step: Name Manager Paste Formulas *fx*

STEP
04
Calculating areas

a. Select cells F5:F13 and label them D. ☐

b. Now go to cell G5 and use **Equation 2** to get the area of the spheres of water if we created a baby planet made of saline water only. Use the diameters of column F and your D name to achieve this, but remember that **Equation 2** is based on radius, so make the necessary adjustment. ☐

c. Copy your G5 formula down to cells G6:G13 but also without screwing up our formatting. ☐

ProTip

Most people understand that their spreadsheets should be functional and automated, but very few spend some time making them look good with color, buttons, comprehensive titles and table headers, and even an appropriate amount of decimal digits in their numbers. Stand out from the crowd!

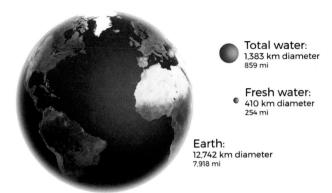

Total water:
1,383 km diameter
859 mi

Fresh water:
410 km diameter
254 mi

Earth:
12,742 km diameter
7,918 mi

Figure 11. The size of the Earth compared to the size of spheres containing only its water (total and freshwater).

Ok, we have completed our table so let us analyze the results. If we took all the water on Earth, whose volume is 1.384 billion km³ (332 million mi³) as shown by cell C13, and made a spherical planet with it, it would have a diameter of 1,383 km (859 mi) and an area of 6,005,913 km² (2,319,888 mi²). To put that in perspective, our Earth has a diameter of 12,742 km (7,918 mi) and an area of around 510,000,000 km² (197,000,000 mi²). As shown in **Figure 11**, our water-only planet is not so big compared to the Earth!

The size of the freshwater sphere looks scary compared to the entire planet and you might start feeling a bit thirsty... 410 km (254 mi) is somewhat the distance between Los Angeles and Las Vegas. Imagine a sphere that size. Now, if you consider that 77% of that water is locked in ice and glaciers mostly in Antarctica, our thirst deepens. In the following step we will put these numbers in perspective once more to avoid the notion that there is not enough water for us and other lovely creatures.

STEP 05
Annual human water needs

a. We know that the recommended consumption of water per capita is 50 liters (13 gallons) **per day**, that there are roughly 7 billion people on Earth (7×10^9), that there are 365 days in one year, and that 1 km³ (0.24 mi³) contains 10^{12} liters (2.65×10^{11} US gallons). With this information, write a formula in cell C20 of your WATER RESOURCES sheet that calculates the total need of water for domestic use in km³ (or mi³ for the Imperial version). ☐

b. In cells D20, D21 and D22 respectively, calculate the percentages that the volumes of water required for domestic use, food production and total human water needs represent compared to the total volume of freshwater. Make sure you use proper references to the cells that contain the information needed to solve this, so that the formula for cell D20 can be copied down. ☐

c. Do the same in cells E20, E21 and E22 but now consider that accessible freshwater includes only lakes and rivers. It looks as if there is indeed enough water for everyone on Earth. The issue is uneven distribution among regions. ☐

d. Complete cells F20:G22 with the proper formulas. You may copy the ones you have used above, but you must make some modifications for them to work due to how the V label was defined. You should be able to do this on your own by now but if not, consider checking the answer key file as a last resort. ☐

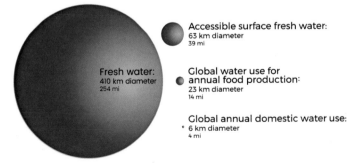

Fresh water:
410 km diameter
254 mi

Accessible surface fresh water:
63 km diameter
39 mi

Global water use for annual food production:
23 km diameter
14 mi

Global annual domestic water use:
6 km diameter
4 mi

Figure 12. Relative size of water spheres compared to total freshwater.

Now let's look at these numbers again. While the amount of freshwater on Earth seems scarce compared to the total amount of water, most of which is in the oceans, the volume of water needed for humans is also small relative to the total amount of accessible freshwater. The spheres of water that would result from these volumes are shown in **Figure 12**.

Wasn't this exercise fantastic? You learned how to type algebraic equations into Excel, strengthened the skills to use names in formulas, and learned a lot about water resources. Your WATER RESOURCES sheet should look like this, with identical values (Imperial screenshot version not shown here, but available in the answer key file):

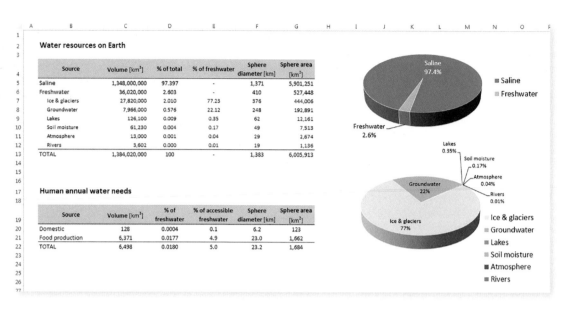

Now we will complete one more example to finish **Part B**. Here you will learn how to add some color images to your Excel spreadsheet so that it stands out from the crowd. I have rarely seen people including images in their files even though their usage makes them look so great.

STEP

06

Inserting
images and
website links

a. Go to the PLANETS sheet of the same file and explore the table. You know where this is going, right? But what about the exaggerated height of the rows? You will soon see! ☐

b. Go to Insert → Pictures and locate the folder **chapter_03_planet_images** that came with your working files, then select **mercury** and Click Insert (you may need to *unzip* the folder first). ☐

c. Once you see the Mercury image embedded in your Excel file, select it to activate the Format tab. On the right of this tab you will see Height and Width boxes, so change the width to 1.5 cm or 0.59 inches (height adjusts automatically). ☐

d. Move the resized Mercury image and locate it properly centered in cell C5. ☐

e. Select the Mercury image and go to Insert → Hyperlink and type this in the Address box: **https://en.wikipedia.org/wiki/Mercury_(planet)**, then Click OK. ☐

f. Click on your Mercury image and, if you have an internet connection, it should take you to the Wikipedia article about this very hot planet. ☐

g. Repeat the procedures above to include all the planet (and moon) images, resize them to 1.5 cm (0.59 inch) in width, place them in the proper cells and link them to their Wikipedia articles. ☐

Buttons used in this step: Pictures 🖳   Hyperlink 🌐

Now let's do some calculations:

STEP

07

Calculating
volume and
area ratios

a. Type a formula in cell E5 that, based on **Equation 1** and Mercury's radius in cell D5, calculates the number of Earths that fit into Mercury (of course you will get a number smaller than 1 for this tiny planet). This formula is a simple ratio dividing the volume of Mercury in km^3 (or mi^3) by the volume of Earth in km^3 (or mi^3). This formula should be robust so that you are able to copy it down to all the planets and the moon, and should result in a value of 1 in cell E7. ☐

b. Do the same to fill column F based on **Equation 2**. ☐

c. Remove all decimals in cells that result in more than one Earth, both for volume and area ratios. ☐

d. Analyze your data: how many Earths fit into Jupiter in terms of volume? How much bigger is the surface of Neptune compared to our planet? ☐

STEP
08
Space tourism

a. Just for fun, calculate the time it would take you to arrive at each planet based on the average speed of a commercial airplane (cell H2) and the distances shown in column G. Note that the speed is given in km/h (mi/h) and you need to specify the travel time in years in cells H5:H13.

b. It is very likely that when you copied the formula you typed in cell H5 to the cells below, you got a #VALUE! error in cell H7 because G7 does not contain a number. Fix this with the very useful =IFERROR( ).

c. Following the same approach and based on cell I2, calculate in cells I5:I13 the number of years it would take to get to the planets and the moon using a traditional space shuttle.

d. You just read that new generation space shuttles travel at a speed of 32,000 km/h (20,000 mi/h), so change that in cell I2 and see how your values in column I change. This is the essence of Excel.

e. Save your file (Ctrl+S).

Your PLANETS sheet should look like this (Imperial version not shown but available in the answer key file):

	Planet	Image*	Radius [km]	Volume [# of Earths]	Area [# of Earths]	Average distance to Earth [km]	Getting there by commercial plane [years]	Getting there by space shuttle [years]
						Speed [km/h]: 1,000		32,000
5	Mercury		2,440	0.06	0.15	91,254,701	10.4	0.3
6	Venus		6,052	0.86	0.90	41,887,404	4.8	0.1
7	Earth		6,371	1.00	1.00	-	-	-
8	Moon		1,738	0.02	0.07	384,400	0.0	0.0
9	Mars		3,397	0.15	0.28	77,790,893	8.9	0.3
10	Jupiter		71,492	1,413	126	628,311,058	71.7	2.2
11	Saturn		60,268	847	89	1,277,565,818	145.8	4.6
12	Uranus		25,559	65	16	2,713,705,380	309.8	9.7
13	Neptune		24,766	59	15	4,347,314,131	496.3	15.5

Planets (and moon)

Part C - Apply your knowledge to a typical example

In this short exercise, you will apply what you have learned so far in a practical example designed for you to build invoices from a list of items. Let's imagine that you are the Store Manager of your pet shop from **Chapter 1**. You will see...

Figure 13. So many products and such vast sales statistics generated through the years. How are you, the Store Manager, going to survive without Excel?

STEP
01
Open, save and
add hyperlinks

a.   Open file **chapter_03_part_C_ invoices_and_sales.xlsx** and save it in a safe location as **chapter_03_part_C_invoices_and_sales_solved.xlsx**. ☐

b.   Explore your file. In the ITEMS sheet you will be able to generate a list of items for a single invoice, which will be automatically summarized in the INVOICES sheet. In other words, by filling data in the ITEMS sheet, many fields of the INVOICES sheet will be filled automatically. You will love this! ☐

c.   You will now learn how to create simple buttons to jump from one sheet to the other, a procedure that makes your simple Excel spreadsheet look like a fancy software interface. Go to cell J2 of your ITEMS sheet and go to Insert → Hyperlink. When the Insert Hyperlink dialog box appears, select Place in This Document from the Link to list and INVOICES from the Cell Reference list under the Or select a place in this document box. Now press the ScreenTip... button and type Go to Invoices in the ScreenTip text box, then Click OK. Click OK again to close the Insert Hyperlink dialog box. ☐

d.   Before clicking the link now created in cell J2, format the cell so that the text goes back to black and not underlined; then locate your cursor in the Formula Bar at the end of the text string (after Invoices), add a space and Click the Symbol button from the Insert tab; choose Wingdings 3 in the Font menu, look for this cute triangle ▶ (character code 117) and Click Insert. ☐

e.   If you accidentally click on your hyperlink of cell J2, don't worry, just go back to your ITEMS sheet and know that you can use the right button of your mouse to select a cell without activating its hyperlink. So select cell J2 again with Right Click and press Ctrl+1 → Border to add a thick border to the bottom and right sides of the cell, then Click OK. Your invoices button should look like this: ☐

f.   Now Click on your Invoices ▶ hyperlink in cell J2. Wooooow! ☐

g.   Repeat the same procedure to cell I2 of your INVOICES sheet to create a button that goes back to the ITEMS sheet, equally formatted but with the cute triangle to the left and with a Screen Tip text that says Back to Items. It should look like this: ☐

h. Make sure both buttons work and, as they do, who needs the sheet tabs in the bottom? Go to File → Options → Advanced and scroll down until you see the Display options for this workbook menu, then deactivate the Show sheet tabs box and Click OK. You are starting to make your spreadsheet look like no one else's. But enough make-up for now; let's do some calculations.

Buttons used in this step: Hyperlink 🌐 Symbol Ω

STEP 02
Creating a functional database

a. Go to your ITEMS sheet and label cells B6:B30 as IPINVOICE (IP at the beginning stands for *item pricing*), cells E6:E30 as IPQUANT, cells F6:F30 as IPPRICEBT, G6:G30 as IPDISC, cells H6:H30 as IPPRICEWD, cells I6:I30 as IPTAX and cells J6:J30 as IPPRICEAT.

b. Go to Formulas → Name Manager → New..., type TAX in the name box and 12% in the Refers to box, then Click OK and close the Name Manager dialog box. This procedure stores the local sales tax value in the TAX name, for us to readily use in formulas with the flexibility of changing it if needed (you wouldn't believe how fiscally unstable some countries are).

c. Now let's list the items of your first two invoices. Type 1 in cells B6, B7 and B8, Labrador dog white + vaccines in cell C6, ACME Blue leash in cell C7 and Dog food + Omega 3 in cell C8. Type 586.20 in cell D6, 28.99 in cell D7 and then 45.80 in cell D8, and then 1 in cell E6, 1 in cell E7 and 3 in cell E8.

d. Now we will combine an *IF* statement with two conditions to get the price before tax for each item, and in the process you will reinforce the use of the logical operator =AND( ) to comply with more than one criterion. In cell F6, type =IF(AND(D6<>"",E6<>""),D6*E6,"---"), which says: *if both cells D6 and E6 are not empty, then multiply them; otherwise show three dashes.*

e. Copy the formula you typed in cell F6 all the way down to reach cell F30 and make cells F6:F30 filled with a very light gray color. By using the formula above with color-coding, we are complying very well with **Best Practices** rule #10, which explains that we should identify cell types according to their functionality. In this case, we are showing that cells in column F are based on formulas, and later you will learn how to protect them from being overwritten.

Buttons used in this step: Name Manager 🗄

STEP 03
Completing your beautiful database

a. If you are familiar with retail, you know that customers always ask for discounts or you offer promotions. Actually, dogs and dog food are for sale this week —the former because it is low season for dog sales and the latter because it is about to expire. In cells G6, G7 and G8 type 20, 0 and 40 respectively.

b. In cell H6, type =IF(AND(F6<>"---",G6<>""),F6-F6*G6/100,"---") and copy it down to reach cell H30. Make sure that you understand what this formula is doing. Basically, by using this logical statement, we ensure that the user of this database does not forget to type the discount because, otherwise, the final price will not show up.

c. Fill cells H6:H30 with the same gray that you used in column F to indicate that a formula is there (you may use the Format Painter button for this purpose).

d. In cell I6, type a formula that works like this: if the contents of cell H6 are different from three dashes, then multiply the value in cell H6 by the number stored in the TAX name, or otherwise produce three dashes. Then copy the formula down and make the cells gray as before.

e. In cell J6, type a formula that adds the Price with discount [$] with the Tax [$] only if the sum can be done (otherwise produce three dashes too). Then copy the formula down and make the cells gray too.

Buttons used in this step: Format Painter 🖌

The top of your Item - pricing database sheet should look like this, with identical values:

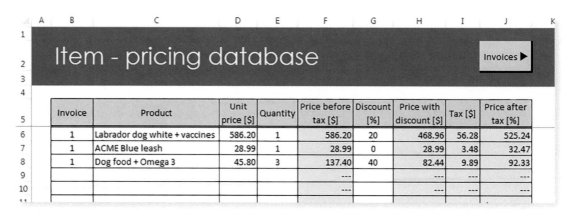

Your database is now fantastic because it visually shows that the user is only supposed to fill data in columns B, C, D, E and G, while everything else is automatically calculated. Now we will add a couple more invoices before moving on, and in the process you will enjoy the pleasure this automation brings to your life.

STEP

04

Adding more
data

a.   Create another invoice (number 2) starting in cell B9, with two items: 1 Siamese cat with   ☐
unit price $655.60 and 25% discount, and 3 bags of Fishy cat food priced $18.99 each with 0%
discount. Wasn't it nice to see the formulas work only if you type in all the data?

b.   Invent invoice 3 on your own, with at least 3 items taken from your imagination, but please be   ☐
reasonable with the prices.

You may have noticed that your Item pricing database is used to display individual items of each invoice, one after the other, but it is limited because, for example, it does not show the total sale per invoice, or the total number of items. So now we will use the Invoice summary database, where each line will represent a single invoice with its totals. To fill it we will use **=COUNTIF( )** and **=SUMIF( )** statements taking advantage of the names we have stored in the Name Manager.

STEP

05

Summarizing
your invoices

a.   Go to your Invoice summary sheet by clicking on your Invoices ▶ button of the Item - pricing   ☐
database. You see that the invoice numbers are pre-written in order, as invoices should be.

b.   In cell D6, type **=SUMIF(IPINVOICE,$B6,IPQUANT)** and understand what the formula is doing.   ☐
Remember what those names represent or check by typing them again in the Name Box.

c.   Use a conditional formatting rule to make the font of 0 values look white and all cells D6:D30   ☐
filled gray as in the other sheet.

d.   Copy the formula of cell D6 to cells E6:I6; they will show the same result but we will now modify   ☐
them one by one. Delete the content of cell F6 as that column will have a special formula.

e.   Go to cell E6 and change the formula to **=SUMIF(IPINVOICE,$B6,IPPRICEBT)**. Notice that you   ☐
are now only changing the third argument of **=SUMIF( )** because they are all based on invoice
numbers.

f.   Modify the formulas in cells G6, H6 and I6 to use the proper names for each field.   ☐

g.   The discount is expressed as a percentage in the Items - pricing database but we need a dollar   ☐
figure in the Invoice summary sheet, so in cell F6 of the Invoice summary sheet type **=E6-G6**,
which is the simplest way of getting that value.

h.   Format cells E6:I6 as numbers with a thousand separator and two decimals, and align them to   ☐
the right.

i.   Propagate the formulas and formats of cells D6:I6 down to row 30.   ☐

j.   Invent some dates for invoices 1, 2 and 3. I will, however, show you a trick to generate today's   ☐
date automatically with a shortcut. We will just assume that invoice #3 was generated today so go

to cell C8 of your Invoice summary database and press Ctrl+; (control and semicolon buttons), then press Enter.

Buttons used in this step: Name Manager 🖨

Your Invoice summary database should look like this (with your own values for invoice #3):

Invoice	Date	Number of items	Price before tax [$]	Discount [$]	Price with discount [$]	Tax [%]	Price after tax [%]
1	2015-07-13	5	752.59	172.20	580.39	69.65	650.04
2	2015-07-15	4	712.57	163.90	548.67	65.84	614.51
3	2015-07-15	3	15,935.00	42.50	15,892.50	1,907.10	17,799.60
4			0	0.00	0.00	0.00	0.00
5			0	0.00	0.00	0.00	0.00
6			0	0.00	0.00	0.00	0.00
7			0	0.00	0.00	0.00	0.00
8			0	0.00	0.00	0.00	0.00
9			0	0.00	0.00	0.00	0.00
10							

Your file is now ready to be used, that is, to receive more data. Please notice that for educational purposes these databases have only 25 rows, but you can create your own with literally thousands of them in a real-life situation. Actually, if you add rows in the middle of your current dataset (e.g. from row 7 to 24), your names will be updated to broaden their range. Test this if you wish by adding rows, copying the formulas and checking the names' extents with the Name Manager.

STEP
06
Playing and final touches

a. Go to your Items - pricing database to invent another invoice (#4) with a few items, and make ☐ sure that all the formulas are working properly. Go to the Invoice summary sheet and notice how your sums have been automatically updated to include invoice #4, and only the date is to be entered. You must be loving this, but wait to see what we do to this file at the end of this book...

b. Do you want to make your file look like real software? We really do not need column and row ☐ headers any longer so go to View in both sheets of your file and uncheck the Headings box.

We are done with **Chapter 3**! You must have learned so much. Using this last exercise as a starting point, in **Chapter 7** you will learn how to make your file error-proof (for example, so that the user cannot skip an invoice or give discounts bigger than 60%). Also, you will protect the cells that contain formulas to prevent your employees from destroying the file by overwriting them. Finally, wouldn't it be nice if you typed a product and the unit price appeared automatically? All of this you will be able to achieve!

5. Review of functions used

=AND( )   =COUNTIF( )   =ROWS( )
=COLUMNS( )   =DATE( )   =SUM( )
=COUNT( )   =IF( )   =SUMIF( )
=COUNTA( )   =IFERROR( )   =SUMIIFS( )
=COUNTBLANK( )   =PI( )

"

Is there really a career which does not require any level of data organization, basic calculations or reporting through graphs? By the end of this book, you will master it all.

CHAPTER 4

Lookup & reference formulas

1. Introduction and learning objectives

In this chapter you will learn more useful Excel functions with emphasis on those in the *lookup & reference* category, as well as a few others. The *lookup & reference* functions are among the most useful and popular, and we use them all the time to comply with our **Best Practices** (especially rule #1). In **Part A** you will learn some specific tricks related to *lookup & reference* formulas, while in **Part B** you will apply these skills to a typical example in the fascinating world of trees, forests and wood. Remember that as you follow these instructions and achieve this chapter's learning objectives, you are becoming a real Excel programmer.

The learning objectives are:

1. Apply *lookup & reference* functions and formulas to solve common exercises.
2. Understand the concept of *relational database* and how to properly share data without retyping or copying.
3. Reinforce the use of *IF* statements for formula consistency.

2. Specific skills

1. **Using *lookup & reference* functions:** retrieving data from one database to the other; finding data to the right or left of a specific field unifying databases; retrieving exact or approximate matches.
2. **Applying robust and efficient formulas** to relate data from different sources.
3. **Dominating the use** of =VLOOKUP( ) and the =MATCH( ) & =INDEX duo together with =IFERROR( ) to produce consistent, error-free formulas.
4. **Understanding the advantages and disadvantages** of specific *lookup & reference* functions.
5. **Identifying the *Best Practices*** applied in this chapter to reinforce their use and deepen their meaning.

3. Background

3.1 Lookup formulas

Lookup formulas simply extract the value from one field in a database which matches the inquired value belonging to another field. In simple words, for instance, a lookup formula could be used to retrieve a person's phone number from a database when searching by last name. This will become very clear as you complete this chapter. There are several functions in Excel that can achieve this, all with advantages and disadvantages. At the end you will learn and apply the functions that are most robust and flexible.

3.2 Relational databases

There are several ways to organize data, and the concept of **relational database** is applicable to **Part B** of this chapter. If you wish, find what a *relational database* is online and think of the concept as you complete the procedures of **Part B**.

4. Procedures

Through the following steps, you will complete all tasks described in **Section 2**, but not necessarily in the same order. Remember our legend convention as you read: **file name**, Excel location (tab, menu, button, dialog box, control, option or cell coordinates), keyboard or mouse button(s), **formula**, typed data and procedure.

Part A - Typical lookup procedures

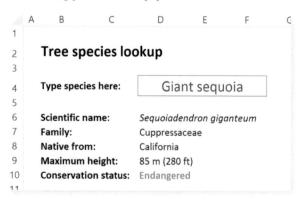

Figure 14. In this lovely Excel file, simply typing **Giant sequoia** in the space provided automatically retrieves the information about the species, shown below. Ready to learn how to do this?

ProTip

The most powerful and versatile way of looking up values from a database is through the **=MATCH( )** and **=INDEX( )** combination. Try using it all the time!

In the following procedures, you will use a few *lookup & reference* functions to perform simple operations:

STEP 01
Open, save, and first vertical lookup exercise (sorted data)

a. Open the file **chapter_04_part_A_lookup.xlsx** and save it in a safe location in your hard drive as **chapter_04_part_A_lookup_solved.xlsx**.

b. Go to the VLOOKUP-sorted sheet. The idea is that if we input any numerical grade in cell F4, a formula will tell us the letter it corresponds to based on the data of cells B5:C15, which have already been labeled GRADES. In cell F5, type **=VLOOKUP(F4,GRADES,2)**, which works this way: look for the value input in cell F4 within the GRADES data and in F5 return the value from the second column of GRADES that is closest to the lookup value in F4.

c. In cell F4 type 77, then 78, and then 80, noticing what happens with the output in cell F5.

d. Now go to cell F5 and using the Formula Bar, put the cursor after the 2 and type a comma. The **=VLOOKUP( )** function has four arguments, but if you leave the fourth blank, it uses an approximate match as default (the same as if **TRUE** is typed as the fourth argument). This means that formula will find the closest value but the data must be sorted in ascending order. This approach is useful when you have sorted data (e.g. retrieving the tax bracket for your income) but useless if you want to find an exact match (e.g. searching for the total sale of invoice #128). The differences will be clearer in the following exercises.

STEP 02
Vertical lookup - exact match

a. In cell H5 of the VLOOKUP-exact sheet type **=VLOOKUP($H$4,$B$5:$E$12,2,FALSE)** (this formula is in the **Select formula index** at the end). As opposed to the formula of the previous example, in which a letter grade would be found for any number, here there must be an exact match between the value you are looking for and a value in the first column of your lookup range. This is achieved by introducing **FALSE** as the fourth argument, which indicates that the formula must find an exact match. Make sure you understand exactly how this formula works and what each argument means.

b. In cell H4, type something random that is not in column B and see what happens. Then type again any of the codes that are in the database so that you do not get an error in cell H5.

c. In cell H6, type **=VLOOKUP($H$4,$B$5:$E$12,3,FALSE)** (or, even better, copy the formula from cell H5 and modify it accordingly).

d. Type a proper formula in cell H7.

e. Play by looking up different codes in cell H4 and enjoying how the other cells change.

f. Sort the data by descending order in price and confirm that the formulas in cells H5:H7 still give you the right values.

By now you must clearly understand how **=VLOOKUP( )** works. Its advantage is flexibility in looking for an approximate match if the data are sorted in ascending order, or for an exact match regardless of data sorting. The disadvantage is that you **must** have the lookup values in the **first** column of your lookup range, and that you have to manually determine the column number within this range where the value you want to retrieve is located. Therefore, **=VLOOKUP( )** is not designed to retrieve values to the left of a given field.

STEP 03
Horizontal lookup

The **=VLOOKUP( )** and **=HLOOKUP( )** functions work in the same way but for vertically- and horizontally- displayed datasets, respectively.

a. Go to the HLOOKUP-exact sheet and in cell Q5, type a formula using **=HLOOKUP( )** that would retrieve the total expenses for a target month specified in Q4. Use the name EXPENSES in your formula, which refers to cells B4:N12.

b. In cell Q4, type Mar and check if your formula in cell Q5 is giving you the right total expense ☐
    for that month.
c. Play around typing different months in cell Q4 and looking at the result in Q5. Make sure you ☐
    understand the logic behind **=HLOOKUP( )** and its arguments.

The **=HLOOKUP( )** function also gives the option of retrieving approximate matches for sorted data; since it
works exactly as **=VLOOKUP( )**, we will just skip that example.

<table>
<tr><td>

STEP
04
IF statement
and lookup
comparison

</td><td>

IF statements based on **=IF( )** or **=IFERROR( )** can be used to allocate specific values according to defined
criteria; however, sometimes too many criteria are needed and therefore lookup functions are easier to apply
for identical results. This is illustrated in the following example. Go to the IF-VLOOKUP comparison sheet,
where 2013 Hydrology final grades are displayed; in the Letter (IF) column we wish to classify the grades in
the different letter grade categories:

</td></tr>
</table>

a. In cell D5 type: **=IF(C5>=90,"A+",IF(C5>=85,"A",IF(C5>=80,"A",IF(C5>=76,"B+",IF(C5>=72,"B** ☐
    ",IF(C5>=68,"B",IF(C5>=64,"C+",IF(C5>=60,"C",IF(C5>=55,"C-",IF(C5>=50,"D","F")))))))))). As
    this formula is so long, you may want to copy it from the eBook (www.excelpro.com) directly
    into your Formula Bar. Despite its length, please understand how it works.
b. **OPTIONAL**: if you are an Excel® 2016 user with an Office® 365 subscription, replace the formula ☐
    in the step above in cell D5 with one based on the **=IFS( )** function, which was introduced in
    this latest version to avoid such long "nested" **=IF( )** formulas. Check the help (F1) to understand
    how the **=IFS( )** function works. Just before you skip this step, consider our **Best Practices** rule
    #9 to avoid virtually all those parentheses needed for **=IFS( )**.
c. Copy the formula down to retrieve the letter grades for all students. ☐
d. In cell E5, use **=VLOOKUP( )** to obtain the same result as in column D, taking advantage of the ☐
    GRADES name of sheet VLOOKUP-sorted.
e. Type any four-digit student number in cell H4 that you see in column B. ☐
f. In cell H5, type a formula that uses **=IFERROR( )** and **=VLOOKUP( )** to display a Hydrology grade ☐
    if a student number is found, or else display Not found (**=VLOOKUP( )** would return a nasty
    error if used alone for such a case).
g. Use a formula that retrieves your letter grade in cell H6, including the **=IFERROR( )** function ☐
    as above.

<table>
<tr><td>

STEP
05
Looking up a
value anywhere
in a range

</td><td>

As you know, one limitation of **=VLOOKUP( )** is that the lookup values must be placed in the first column
of the lookup range. There are two options to look for values in cases where your lookup column is not the
first or is even to the right of the values to be retrieved. Go to the BEST LOOKUP sheet, where we want to
retrieve Price and fuel efficiency in L/100 km and mi/gal (for Imperial users) based on a car's make and model.
The first option is to use **=LOOKUP( )** in vector mode, but that function does not work when you change
the sorting of the data, so we will go straight to the most robust, versatile and fantastic way of performing
lookups which is to combine **=INDEX( )** and **=MATCH( )**.

</td></tr>
</table>

a. In cell I6, type: **=INDEX(PRICE,MATCH(I$4,MAKEMODEL,0))** (this formula is in the **Select** ☐
    formula index at the end). Read the help for **=INDEX( )** and **=MATCH( )** to make perfect sense
    of what this formula is about, noticing what the PRICE and MAKEMODEL names refer to.
b. Fill in the proper formula for cells I7 and I8 (copy the formula from cell I6 and just change what ☐
    you need to change).
c. Play around with make and model names in cell I4 to see how your formulas work. ☐
d. Add an **=IFERROR( )** component to your formulas in cells I6, I7 and I8 so that Not found is ☐
    displayed when a make & model not on the list is searched for in cell I4.

Part B – Applied exercise

Have you ever wondered where wood comes from? From trees, of course, but certainly not from those growing in the park. Since wood is such a key and irreplaceable raw material for humanity, providing everything from houses to toilet paper, the forestry industry is as important as the food industry. Some countries are better wood producers than others, and timber may originate from trees extracted from natural forests with minimum ecological impact, vast plantations established and cultivated entirely by and for people, but also, unfortunately, from destructive illegal deforestation. Despite their bad reputation, most forestry companies do a great job to manage their forests in a sustainable way, while deforestation is mostly attributable to land clearing for agriculture or urban development.

In this exercise, you will be the manager of a forestry company in charge of a big piece of land divided into smaller lots that foresters call *stands*. In human-established forest plantations, each *stand* is a continuous area with the same tree species, planted at the same time and for the same purpose —such as producing paper pulp in the shortest time possible. **Figure 15** shows part of your company's land and three examples of pine stands with their close-ups.

Figure 15. Example of three forest stands of different ages and species (delineated with light green). Tree diameters and heights need to be recorded from a sample of trees in each stand in order to estimate the total volume of wood that you can harvest.

Your company owns a mill that processes the timber and to ensure enough supply in the long term, you need to have forest plantations of all ages to reach annual harvesting targets. Foresters require this long-term vision because trees take many years to grow: what you plant today will be used in 20 years or more, depending on the region. To measure how much wood they have in their forests, companies conduct inventories where a sample of trees in each stand (you cannot possibly measure them all!) is assessed to obtain diameters and heights (see **Figure 15**). With this information, individual tree timber volume can be estimated and then extrapolated to obtain stand-level totals. At the end of the day, it is this volume of wood that matters to the forester —not leaves or branches— in the same way that the butcher is interested in steak —not hair or bones. In this long process, however, forests must be properly planted, weed-controlled, pruned, thinned, and protected from disease and fire before harvesting takes place when trees are mature.

After this brief lesson in forestry, you are ready to complete this interesting exercise, where you will work with multiple databases containing very detailed information about all the stands managed by your forestry company. Lookup formulas will be used to retrieve relevant figures from one database to the other. This exercise is of critical importance as so many daily-life examples require the same approach. The file used in this **Part B** is a fantastic model of how you should organize your databases applying many of our ***Best Practices***.

STEP
01
Open, save and name

a. Open the file **chapter_04_part_B_relational_databases.xlsx** and save it in a safe location as **chapter_04_part_B_relational_databases_solved.xlsx**. If you wish to work with this file in Imperial units, make sure you use the version **chapter_04_part_B_relational_databases_imperial. xlsx**. Browse through the sheets. You notice that there are different types of information for forest stands in the various sheets, and that you cannot possibly put them together in a single sheet given the amount of information. Interestingly, you also realize that all the databases in the different sheets begin with the Stand code in the first column, so this is an ideal situation to use **=VLOOKUP( )** to retrieve data from one sheet to the other based on this common field for all. Also, it is important for you to know that all the surfaces are in hectares [ha] (or acres). Tree diameters are measured in centimeters [cm] (or inches [in]), tree heights in meters [m] (or feet [ft]), and tree volumes in cubic meters [m^3] (or cubic feet [ft^3]). Aggregated volumes are also often expressed in cubic meters per hectare [m^3/ha] (or cubic feet per acre [ft^3/acre]).

b. Go to the GENERAL sheet, select all cells in the database (B5:O443) and label them GENERAL in the Name Box.

c. Go to the INVESTMENTS sheets and label cells B5:J189 INVEST in the Name Box.

d. Go to the MENSURATION sheet and label cells B5:M285 MENSUR.

e. Go to the FIRES sheet and label cells B5:G452 FIRES.

f. In the ROADS sheet, label cells B5:G478 ROADS.

g. Go to the GENERAL sheet and type 1 in cell B1, type 2 in cell C1, 3 in cell D1 and so on (auto fill this quickly) until you reach 14 in cell O1.

h. Select cells B1:O1 in the GENERAL sheet and make the font color white so that the numbers that you generated are hidden.

i. Repeat this procedure in all other sheets, where you are essentially numbering each column in row 1 and making those numbers white. You will later see why this will help us.

STEP
02
Completing the GENERAL database

a. Type the formula **=IFERROR(VLOOKUP($B5,ROADS,ROADS!$G$1,FALSE),"-")** in cell D5 of the GENERAL sheet and copy it down to fill column D; understand exactly what it is doing because you will be applying this a lot.

b. The Net surface [ha] (or Net surface [acres]) is the surface occupied by trees only within each stand, defined as the difference between Total surface [ha] (Total surface [acres]) and Total road surface [ha] (Total road surface [acres]) so fill the cells in column E with the proper formula.

c. Fill cells in columns J to M in our range by retrieving the corresponding values from the MENSUR database (use the same logic as for column E); notice that the Total timber volume [m^3] (Total timber volume [ft^3]) column has no data yet and the formula is producing zeros where there are blanks in the MENSURATION database; don't worry about this for now because we will fix it later. If you copied and pasted formulas to do this, make sure that your data in the GENERAL sheet has the same number of decimals as in the corresponding databases where you retrieved the information.

d. Fill the cells of columns N and O in your GENERAL sheet with information obtained from the INVESTMENT and FIRES sheets, respectively (use your names). ☐

a. Go to the INVESTMENTS database and using one single formula that retrieves the stands' net surface from the GENERAL database, fill cells J5:J189; don't forget to display dashes instead of errors. ☐

b. Go to the MENSURATION sheet and complete column H with a single formula that estimates mean tree Height growth [m/year] (Height growth [ft/year]); for this task you will be using the Mean tree height [m] (Mean tree height [ft]) data, the date of height measurement clearly indicated in the Height updated as of column, and the stands' Plantation date of the GENERAL database (use 365.25 as the mean number of days per year and don't forget dashes instead of errors, last time I remind you!). For this step, you might want to build your formula from the inside out, first retrieving the plantation date, then subtracting it from the height measurement date, then dividing that by 365.25 to get the time elapsed in years, then dividing the tree height by this number of years, and finally applying =IFERROR( ) to it all. ☐

c. Fill the Total timber volume [m³] (Total timber volume [ft³]) and Volume yield [m³/ha/year] (Volume yield [ft³/acre/year]) columns with proper, robust formulas (use Net surface [ha] or Net surface [acre]). Hint: to complete Volume yield [m³/ha/year] (Volume yield [ft³/acre/year]), just copy the formula you used for Height growth [m/year] (Height growth [ft/year]) and modify it. ☐

The upper part of your three completed sheets should look like this (Imperial unit version not shown but available in the corresponding answer key file):

General database

Stand	Total surface [ha]	Total road surface [ha]	Net surface [ha]	Type	Species	Mean elevation [m]	Plantation date	Number of trees per hectare [n/ha]	Mean tree diameter [cm]	Mean tree height [m]	Total timber volume [m³]	Total investment [US$]	Fire risk
0100 A2	31.75	0.24	31.51	Commercial plantation	Pine	3,291	2006-06	1,655	-	0.3	-	12,440	Moderate
0100 E1	0.58	0.00	0.58	Trial	Pine	3,348	1983-04	2,180	21.5	18.3	369.9	0	High
0100 R	5.45	0.00	5.45	Protected area	-	3,277	-	-	-	-	-	-	Extreme
0101 A2	18.17	0.29	17.88	Commercial plantation	Pine	3,211	2006-05	2,109	-	-	-	6,825	Moderate
0101 R	9.61	0.02	9.59	Protected area	-	3,195	-	-	-	-	-	-	Extreme
0102 A1	43.59	0.86	42.73	Commercial plantation	Pine	3,167	1989-04	761	27.7	21.2	13,645.8	-	Moderate
0102 C1	1.77	0.14	1.63	Commercial plantation	Pine	3,184	1989-04	467	35.1	25.0	703.1	-	Moderate
0102 H1	1.67	0.00	1.67	Seed orchard	Pine	3,160	1988-06	253	42.4	20.2	561.5	-	Moderate
0102 I	2.19	0.10	2.09	Infrastructure	-	3,156	-	-	-	-	-	-	Low
0102 R	3.29	0.00	3.29	Protected area	-	3,156	-	-	-	-	-	-	Extreme
0102 S1	1.77	0.00	1.77	Trial	Several species	3,144	1990-04	-	-	-	-	-	High

Investments

Stand	Land preparation [US$]	Plantation [US$]	Maintenance [US$]	Thinning + prunning [US$]	Protection [US$]	Others [US$]	Total investment [US$]	Investment [US$/ha]
0100 E1	0.00	0.00	0.00	0.00	0.00	0.00	0.00	0.00
0106 B1	0.00	0.00	0.00	208.26	0.00	0.00	208.26	191.06
0200 A1	0.00	0.00	0.00	687.18	0.00	0.00	687.18	91.75
0200 B2	0.00	0.00	679.62	0.00	0.00	0.00	679.62	26.65
0201 A2	0.00	0.00	139.01	363.93	0.00	0.00	502.94	97.28
0201 B2	0.00	0.00	138.84	334.14	0.00	0.00	472.98	211.15
0201 D2	0.00	0.00	741.41	919.40	0.00	0.00	1,660.81	158.02
0202 A2	0.00	0.00	308.92	1,304.23	0.00	0.00	1,613.15	138.83
0202 B1	0.00	0.00	0.00	519.79	0.00	0.00	519.79	91.35

	A	B	C	D	E	F	G	H	I	J	K	L	M	N
1														
2		**Mensuration data**												
3														
4		Stand	Trees per hectare	Trees per hectare updated as of	Mean tree diameter [cm]	Tree diameter updated as of	Mean tree height [m]	Height growth [m/year]	Height updated as of	Volume [m³/ha]	Total timber volume [m³]	Volume yield [m³/ha/year]	Volume updated as of	
5		0100 E1	2,180	2006-04-04	21.5	2006-04-04	18.3	0.80	2006-04-04	638	370	27.8	2006-04-04	
6		0102 A1	761	2007-02-02	27.7	2007-02-02	21.2	1.19	2007-02-02	319	13,646	18.0	2007-02-02	
7		0102 C1	467	2007-02-07	35.1	2007-02-07	25.0	1.41	2007-02-07	431	703	24.3	2007-02-07	
8		0102 H1	253	2007-03-05	42.4	2007-03-05	20.2	1.08	2007-03-05	336	562	18.0	2007-03-05	
9		0104 A1	644	2006-12-06	29.1	2006-12-06	21.3	1.03	2006-12-06	318	13,061	15.5	2006-12-06	
10		0104 B1	550	2007-02-02	29.9	2007-02-02	26.8	1.29	2007-02-02	364	2,099	17.6	2007-02-02	
11		0105 A1	712	2006-12-04	26.3	2006-12-04	18.2	0.93	2006-12-04	269	8,995	13.7	2006-12-04	
12		0106 A1	545	2006-12-04	15.6	2006-12-04	12.0	0.49	2006-12-04	130	1,468	5.3	2006-12-04	
13		0106 B1	580	2006-12-04	27.9	2006-12-04	15.7	0.89	2006-12-04	252	275	14.3	2006-12-04	
14		0107 A1	550	2007-02-02	7.6	2007-02-02	6.4	0.36	2007-02-02	9	187	0.5	2007-02-02	

STEP

04

Individual stand consultation and best practices review

a.   Complete the INDIVIDUAL STAND sheet so that you can consult the data of a user-defined target stand to be entered in cell C4. Make sure the formulas produce Not found for stands not in the list.   ☐

b.   Go to the BEST PRACTICES sheet and complete the table about the use of ***Best Practices*** in our work. Simply type the rule number in the first column of the table and very briefly describe how we are applying each rule in this chapter (only consider applicable rules, and feel free to give examples). If you feel lazy, check the answer key file, but do not skip this procedure.   ☐

We are done with **Chapter 4**! Congratulations! Now you will take a very well-deserved break from functions and formulas in the next two chapters.

5. Review of functions used

=HLOOKUP( )
=IF( )
=IFERROR( )
=IFS( )
=INDEX( )
=LOOKUP( )
=MATCH( )
=VLOOKUP( )

CHAPTER 5

Creating beautiful charts

1. Introduction and learning objectives

Creating professional charts is extremely important: most people do not really read papers as much as they look at their graphs. Excel is a fantastic —and probably the most widely used— software to create all sorts of charts. In this chapter you will learn all the basics of charts and how to comply with the *Best Practices* rule #4. In **Part A** you go in detail through each type of pre-made chart options offered by Excel, while in **Part B** you will apply your knowledge to a simple and very short exercise.

The learning objectives are:

1. Become familiar with the different chart types offered by Excel.
2. Understand the importance of producing beautiful and functional charts.
3. Identify the best type of chart for a specific purpose.
4. Maximize the aesthetic and professional appearance of charts.
5. Minimize the time it takes to create and modify charts.

2. Specific skills

1. **Generating the most popular chart types**: area, bar, column, line, pie, special pie, scatter, and bubble.
2. Setting up data for correct graphic display.
3. **Producing aesthetic and complete charts**: understanding the importance of producing good-looking, self-explanatory charts.
4. **Editing charts**: colors, borders, legends, axes, titles and gridlines.
5. **Copying chart formatting** from one to the other.
6. **Understanding primary and secondary axes** in compound charts.
7. **Adding and removing data** to an existing chart.
8. **Inserting elements into charts** (e.g. shapes and textboxes).
9. **Combining chart types**: creating compound charts that, for example, combine lines with columns.
10. **Modifying axis scales**: manually editing axis scales to improve the appearance of a chart.
11. **Creating grayscale charts** to avoid printing issues.

3. Background

3.1 Definition and importance of charts

Charts are graphical representations of data, and their importance cannot be overemphasized. Just as an action is worth a thousand words and an image works much better than a poem to depict a landscape, charts can be many times better than tables with numbers. It is extremely important for professionals to be able to produce excellent charts, and Excel is probably the best tool to achieve this.

3.2 Excel and charts

Excel® 2013 significantly improved the interface for producing charts and the default settings, which required much more editing in Excel® 2010 and earlier. All charts come from properly structured data, so pay attention to how the data are organized while you complete the following steps. Also, feel free to play with the many options that Excel offers in terms of styles and displayed information. An important part of this chapter is that you understand what is the best type of graph to match a particular dataset. For example, line charts are adequate for data that change over time, while pie charts are preferred when showing percentages. Charts are worth a thousand words!

4. Procedures

Through the following steps, you will complete all tasks described in **Section 2**, but not necessarily in the same order. Remember our legend convention as you read: **file name**, Excel location (tab, menu, button, dialog box, control, option or cell coordinates), keyboard or mouse button(s), **formula**, typed data and procedure.

Part A - Chart types

In this first part you will learn how to create charts of most types offered by Excel, such as the ones shown in **Figure 16**, as well as some editing tricks necessary to make them look gorgeous.

STEP
01
Area charts

a. Open the file **chapter_05_part_A_chart_types. xlsx** and save it in a safe location as **chapter_05_ part_A_chart_types_solved.xlsx**. Use the **chapter_05_part_A_chart_types_imperial.xlsx** if you wish to work with Imperial units.   ☐

b. **Excel® 2013 users**: go to the AREA sheet, select cells B4:G11, go to Insert → Chart → Click on the Insert Area Chart option and in the **2-D Area** section, select Stacked Area. **Excel® 2016 users**: go to the AREA sheet, select cells B4:G11, go to Insert → Insert Line or Area Chart → 2-D Area → Stacked Area (second option)   ☐

Figure 16. Regardless of your career, whether in the social or natural sciences, you will always need to produce charts. Excel is the way to go, as you are about to experience.

c. You realize that it is not practical to show the *y-axis* in actual number of people because the billions take so much space to display. Select the *y-axis* numbers, then Right Click → Format Axis, and in the menu displayed on the right, under Axis Options → Axis Options (bars button on the right) select Millions in the Display units box. Manually delete the Millions text that appears to the left of the numbers. We will take care of that later.

d. Right Click over the Plot Area of the graph and select Format Plot Area; in the menu displayed on the right under Fill & Line → Border choose Solid line → Color → Black.

e. Right Click on the *y-axis* numbers, select Format Axis → Axis Options (right of the screen) → Fill & Line → Line → Solid line → Color → Black.

f. Do the same for the *x-axis* so that all lines in the graph are regular plain simple black. Following **Best Practices** rule #4, we need to make our graph absolutely self-explanatory with clear units, axis titles and chart title.

g. Go to the Design tab of the Chart Tools menu that appears when your chart is selected; Click on Add Chart Element → Axis Titles → Primary Horizontal, and then manually edit the title that appears by typing Year.

h. Now go to Add Chart Element → Axis Titles → Primary Vertical and edit the vertical title to say Millions of people.

i. Change the font size of both the vertical and horizontal axis titles to 12.

j. Edit the default Chart Title in your graph to World population by continent.

k. The legend at the bottom, displaying the colors for Africa, Americas, etc., is wasting valuable space in the graph: select the legend and move it with the mouse inside the Plot Area, in the upper space (rectangle formed by the 7,000 - 8,000 left axis scale).

l. Select the Plot Area and increase its size with the mouse so that it now fills the entire Chart Area, occupying the space at the bottom previously dedicated to the legend.

m. Right Click on the graph → Format Chart Area → Chart Options → Fill & Line → Fill → No fill, and then Border → No line.

n. Select your entire chart and through the Home tab make all fonts plain black (the default is gray, for some reason).

o. Select your graph and in the Format tab, type 13 cm (or 5.11 inch) in the Width box to the right. Your graph is done! It should look like this:

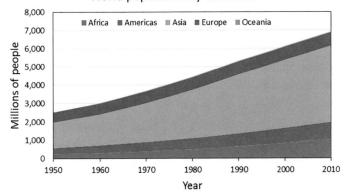

p. Click on your graph, copy and paste it below to create a duplicate (you need to place the cursor in a cell in the worksheet before pasting; if you paste while the graph is still selected the data will be duplicated within the graph); then Right Click on this duplicate and select Change Chart Type and in the Area options choose the 3-D Area (fourth option), then Click OK.

q. Modify the graph so that it looks good (legend properly centered) and eliminate the O... A... and A... axis marks on the right since we cannot see them and we are already using the colored legend to identify continents.

r. Now, this type of graph needs reordering of the continents since Europe and Oceania are behind giant Asia. Right Click on any of the data polygons and choose Select Data..., then select Europe with the mouse and using the arrows to the right of the Legend Entries (Series) box, move it so that it appears before Africa; then put Oceania in the very first place.

s. Select both graphs in your AREA sheet and go to the Page Layout tab → Align → Align left. Your second graph should look like this:

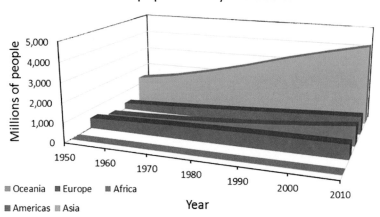

Buttons used in this step: Insert Line or Area Chart 〰 Add Chart Element ⬛

STEP

02

Bar charts

a. **Excel® 2013 users**: go to the BAR sheet and select the entire range containing data, then go to Insert tab → Insert Bar Chart → Clustered Bar (very first option). **Excel® 2016 users**: go to the BAR sheet and select the entire range containing data, then go to Insert tab → Insert Column or Bar Chart → Clustered Bar (first option under 2-D Bar).

b. Look at the resulting graph... You immediately notice that it looks a bit busy and hard to interpret. It is very common for us to choose a chart option that is not the best at first and, while usually there is no right or wrong graph for a specific purpose, we can try to select the best alternative from the many available.

c. Right Click on your graph → Change Chart Type → Bar → 3-D 100% Stacked Bar → OK. Much better! But not there yet... There are many things we can do to this graph so that it tells the story we want to tell.

d. Add a Primary Horizontal axis title that displays Percentage of respondents (n = 1,250) and change its font to size 12 and bold. Edit the Chart Title default to say Customer satisfaction survey results and make it bold.

e. Right Click between any of the bars, select 3-D Rotation and activate the Right Angle Axes box in the right, then set X Rotation to 30° and Y Rotation to 15°.

f. Modify the size of the chart and its elements for a harmonious layout. I would personally increase the chart's width, move the legend to the right and display its categories vertically.

g. Right Click on the Back Wall (just outside the chart bars) and select Format Walls... → Wall Options → Border → Solid line and select a gray color that matches the other lines in the graph. The color scheme of our charts should be useful and help us tell the story the graph is trying to illustrate. In this case, we could choose colors that reflect the survey opinions.

h. Select the *y-axis* legend, then Right Click → Add Major Gridlines.

i. Right Click on any of the bars inside the graph, then Format Data Series... and in the Series Options → Series Options → select 100% for the Gap Width.

j. Select the bars corresponding to the Good category in the graph and Right Click → Format Data Series → Fill → Solid fill and then choose a tone of blue slightly lighter than the one used for the Excellent category; then choose a very light gray for the Neutral category, a light (pinkish) red for the Bad and a darker red for the Terrible category.

k. Make all the text elements in the graph plain black instead of weak gray.

l. Get rid of the Chart Area border as you did for the area graphs above. What a beautiful graph!!!

m. This is not just about beauty, so we must analyze your data. The first thing standing out is your need to change the coffee supplier.

n. Let's remember how our first chart looked: select the data range in cells B4:G11 again and repeat procedure a above by inserting a Clustered Bar graph. Review the differences between the two graphs and appreciate the fact that you live in the 21st Century when it only took a couple of minutes to make a graph look so professional. Your good graph in this sheet must look like the one below and you should almost feel like eating its bars; they look delicious and if you bring your nose to the screen, you will notice they smell nice too:

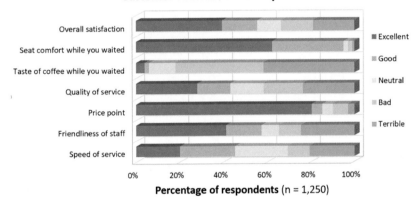

Customer satisfaction survey results

Buttons used in this step: Insert Column or Bar Chart

STEP
03
Column charts

a. **Excel® 2013 users**: go to the COLUMN sheet and select the entire range containing data, then go to Insert tab → Insert Column Chart → 2-D Column → Clustered Column (very first option).
Excel® 2016 users: go to the COLUMN sheet and select the entire range containing data, then go to Insert tab → Insert Column or Bar Chart → 2-D Column → Clustered Column (very first option).

b. As by now you know how to edit charts, first remove the gridlines and then complete the procedures below:

c. Move the legend inside the Plot Area and resize the Plot Area so that it better covers the space available in the entire chart.

d. Change the title to Pet sales by weekday (2013) in font size 14.

e. Add a vertical axis saying Pets sold.

f. Remove the chart's borders (it is very distasteful to submit a chart with borders to a peer-reviewed journal).

g. Manually adjust the chart's elements so that they are harmoniously displayed.

h. Right Click on a column of any of the two products in the graph, then Format Data Series → Fill & Lines → Fill → Gradient fill and explore all the options there until you pick a color and gradient pattern that is pleasing to your eye (make sure you understand how the gradient fill works and the different settings for the direction of the gradient, color, angles, etc.).

i. Then do the same for the other product and your graph is done! It should look like this (with your own color scheme):

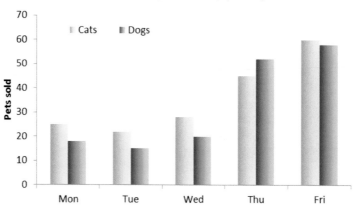

j. Based on the column chart that you just produced, use the copy-paste + Change Chart Type... trick to immediately produce these graphs in the same sheet: Stacked Column, 3-D 100% Stacked Column (in that chart remember to change the *y-axis* title to Percentage), 3-D Cylinder and Full Pyramid (for the last two options you need to start with a 3-D Column chart and change the shape of the columns; you figure it out!). In all cases, make graphs look nice with chart elements aesthetically located, like these:

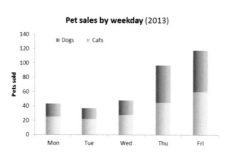
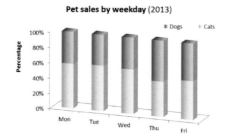
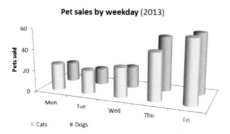
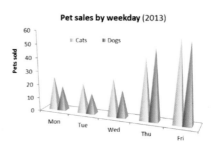

Buttons used in this step: Insert Column or Bar Chart

STEP
04
Line charts

a. Go to the LINE sheet, where US and Canadian dollar exchange rates are shown, and select all the range containing the data there. **Excel® 2013 users:** go to Insert → 2-D Line → Line (very first option). **Excel® 2016 users:** go to Insert tab → Insert Line or Area Chart → 2-D Line → Line (very first option). Make the following edits to the defaults that appear:

b. Edit the chart title to read Daily 2015 exchange rate (US$/CAD) and make it all bold except for the (US$/CAD) at the end.

c. Select the Plot Area border in a gray that matches the rest of the graph.

d. Remove the chart's borders.

e. Make the *y-axis* numbers appear with two decimals only by selecting those numbers, then Right Click → Format Axis... → Axis Options → Axis Options → Number → Decimal places → 2.

f. Right Click on the *x-axis* dates → Format Axis... → Axis Options → Axis Options → Number → Format Code → write mmm d in the box and Click Add.

g. In the same Format Axis dialog box, go to Axis Options and in Major box type 1 and Months again (the Auto to the right should disappear).

h. Right Click on the *x-axis* dates and select Add Major Gridlines.

i. Select the Plot Area → Right Click → Format Plot Area... → Fill → Solid fill → Color and pick the lightest baby blue that you find in the defaults and set the Transparency to 55%. Wow, subtly elegant.

j. Make all text plain black, and the plot area borders and axis lines black too. You also need to find out how to add black tick marks to your *y-axis* values.

k. Change the font size of your *y-axis* numbers and the dates in the *x-axis* to 12. If you always take this little time to improve the appearance of your graphs like we are doing here, everyone who sees them will be really impressed. The other line chart options in the menu do not add much value or excitement so we will keep this one, which should look like this:

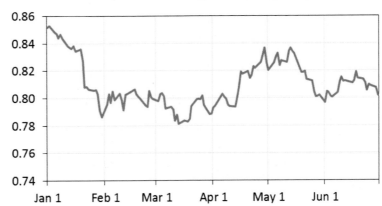

Daily 2015 exchange rate (US$/CAD)

Buttons used in this step: Insert Line or Area Chart

STEP
05
Pie charts

a. Go to the PIE sheet and select the range containing data there and go to Insert tab → Insert Pie or Doughnut Chart → Pie (very first option under 2-D Pie). Make the following edits to the default that appeared:

b. Edit the title to say Preferred car brands.

c. Go to the Design tab under the Chart Tools tab from the Chart Styles and select the very last one (Style 12), which looks 3-D (you must use the down arrow to go to the second row of styles).

d. Remove the chart's border.

e.   Change the font size of the legend to 12.   ☐
                                                                                                  ☐
f.   Go to Design → Quick Layout and select the first option, which displays brands and percentages.   ☐
     Sometimes these quick pre-designed options are useful.

g.   Select the legends that you just displayed (Mazda 14%, etc.), and make them white **Arial bold**   ☐
     font size 10.

h.   Select the Plot Area and enlarge it so that it better fits the chart.   ☐

i.   Right Click over the pie slices → Format Data Series... and increase the Pie Explosion value to   ☐
     7%. Explore other options in the Format Data Series... There are so many things that you can
     do. Your chart should look like this:

Buttons used in this step: Insert Pie or Doughnut Chart 🥧

Go to the SPECIAL PIE sheet which contains the Earth's water volume in km^3 according to different
sources, where all categories other than saline represent freshwater (you used these data in **Chapter
3**). A normal pie chart is inconvenient because some of the categories would not be visible due to
their small relative scale.

a.   Select the range containing data, then go to Insert tab → Insert Pie or Doughnut Chart → Pie   ☐
     of Pie (second option under 2-D Pie).

b.   Right Click on the pie slices → Format Data Series... and in the Values in second plot box type   ☐
     6. Make sure you understand what we just did. In the following procedures we will make some
     important edits.

c.   Edit the chart title to say Distribution of global water resources in black bold.   ☐

d.   Remove the chart's borders.   ☐

e.   Right Click on the slices and select Add Data Labels → Add Data Labels. Then Right Click   ☐
     on those data labels in the chart → Format Data Labels... → Label Options → and activate the
     Percentage box only, deactivating all the rest. Also, in the Number menu below display these
     data labels as a percentage with one decimal. Make all of them black and, finally, delete those
     that appear as 0.0% manually, one by one. You notice that, still, some of the categories are too
     small to be seen. We will now make another graph that does not include saline water.

f.   Copy and paste your graph somewhere else in the sheet; select this second graph and resize the   ☐
     purple and blue rectangles in the data source with your mouse to exclude Saline water.

g.   Right Click on the pie slices → Format Data Series... and in the Values in second plot box type 4.   ☐

h.   Change the title of this second graph to Distribution of global freshwater resources.   ☐

i.   Re-insert all Data Labels so that none are missing and format all as percentages with two   ☐
     decimals. Done with the special pie charts!!! They should look like this:

Distribution of global water resources

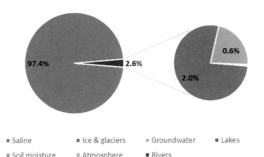

- Saline
- Ice & glaciers
- Groundwater
- Lakes
- Soil moisture
- Atmosphere
- Rivers

Distribution of global freshwater resources

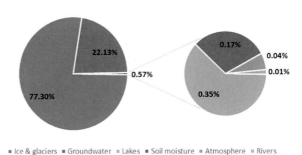

- Ice & glaciers
- Groundwater
- Lakes
- Soil moisture
- Atmosphere
- Rivers

Buttons used in this step: Insert Pie or Doughnut Chart

STEP
07
Scatter charts

Scatter charts are specifically used to visualize the relationship between two variables. We will review them more thoroughly in **Chapter 8**, but let's take a quick look at how to create them here.

a. Go to the SCATTER sheet where a list of individual pine trees is displayed and select the Tree diameter [cm] (Tree diameter [in]) and Height [m] (Height [ft]) data only, then go to Insert tab → Insert Scatter (X, Y) or Bubble Chart → Scatter (very first option). Make the following edits: ☐

b. Edit the chart title to say Diameter - height relationship (*Pinus radiata*) (italics for *Pinus radiata*). ☐

c. Add a Primary Vertical Axis that says Height [m] (Height [ft]) and a Primary Horizontal Axis that says Diameter [cm] (Diameter [in]), making both font size 12. ☐

d. Remove the chart's borders and decimals in both axes. ☐

e. Select the data points in the chart, then Right Click → Format Data Series... → Series Options → Fill & Line → Marker → Marker Options → Built-in and select circle size 4. Then immediately below choose Solid fill in plain black, and No line under Border. The graph shows that as tree diameter increases, height increases too. This is obvious and expected, but notice that there is a lot of variation in the data. A tree can be 45 cm (18 in) in diameter but range in height from 17 to 35 m (56 to 114 ft)! **Chapter 8** will expand on the use of scatter graphs. ☐

f. You will now learn how to move data freely within a graph, which is especially useful to explore relationships between many variables in scatter charts. Select your chart and copy and paste it below (don't forget to Click on a cell after using Ctrl+C and before Ctrl+V). ☐

g. Edit the title of this second chart to be Diameter - height relationship (*Pinus radiata*), and the vertical axis title to be Volume [m³] (Volume [ft³]). To just make the 3 in superscript style, select it individually and press Ctrl+1 → Superscript (yes, you should take the time to do this to be professional in this competitive era). ☐

ProTip

Always take your time to create full self-explanatory headings in your database; write **Temperature [°C]** instead of **Temp** or **Distance [km]** as opposed to **Dist**. Otherwise you may not have a clue what your data represent when you open the file months later.

h. Select the data points in this second graph and you will see how the source data columns appear highlighted (purple for the *x-axis* data and blue for the *y-axis* data). Now move the blue column with the mouse so that it grabs the Volume [m³] (Volume [ft³]) data in column E. By copying and pasting an existing graph, later to be edited, you avoid reformatting everything all over again. Your scatter graphs should look like these:

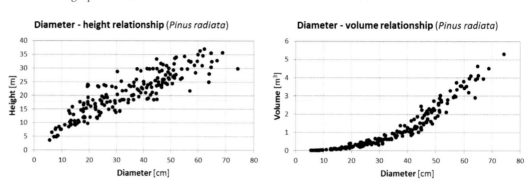

Buttons used in this step: Insert Scatter (X,Y) or Bubble Chart ⠿

STEP
08
Bubble charts

Bubble charts are fun: they are like x-y scatter plots but they also depict a third variable represented by the size of the data points. Go to the BUBBLE sheet, where data of CO_2 emissions by country are accompanied by wealth (GDP per capita), Infant mortality rate and Birth rate.

a. Select cells C5:E83 (data of first three columns; otherwise the chart will not work), then go to Insert tab → Insert Scatter (X, Y) or Bubble Chart → 3-D Bubble (very last option).

b. Make the edits necessary so that it looks like the one below (hint: you need to add a textbox for the bubble size legend explanation and little white squares to hide the negative values in the axis scale):

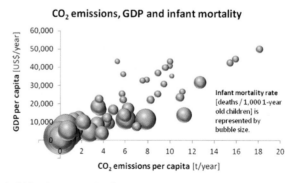

c. Create another bubble chart, equally formatted, that now shows birth rate as bubble size instead of infant mortality. Your chart should look like this (you can pick your own colors):

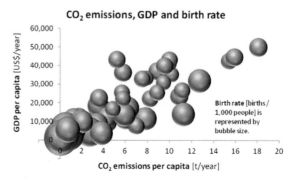

Buttons used in this step: Insert Scatter (X,Y) or Bubble Chart

You are already an expert in producing graphs of different types. Now you will learn a few additional advanced tricks, namely: combining chart types, using a secondary axis scale, adding and removing data series and creating nice black & white graphs.

STEP
09
Combining
charts and
adding a
secondary axis

a. Go to the COMPOUND CHARTS sheet and create a 2-D Clustered Column chart that shows months on the x-axis and clustered columns for both Rainfall [mm] (Rainfall [in]) and Mean temperature [°C] (Mean temperature [°F]) for each month. Your resulting graph is not ideal: both variables share the same *y-axis* and precipitation magnitudes are much higher, so we lose detail of how temperatures are changing; also, while precipitation is adequately represented by columns (resembling rain accumulation), temperature is better illustrated by a line. At least we got the colors right on this first trial! ☐

b. First move the legend to the top of the graph and resize the Plot Area so that it occupies the entire Chart Area. ☐

c. Right Click on the temperature columns → Change Series Chart Type... → Combo and select Line for the Mean temperature [°C] (Mean temperature [°F]) field. And right there activate the Secondary Axis box for temperature too, then Click OK. Yay yay yay! ☐

d. If you are working with metric units, remove the decimals from both the primary and secondary *x-axes* and add axis titles to both saying Precipitation [mm] and Temperature [°C] respectively. If you are working with Imperial units, leave one decimal for the Precipitation [in] axis and no decimals for the Temperature [°F] axis. ☐

e. Remove the Chart Area border, as always. ☐

f. Edit the chart title to Monthly climatic data (Quesnel, BC, 545 m) or Monthly climatic data (Quesnel, BC, 1,788 ft) if using Imperial units. ☐

g. Aesthetically resize and move your chart and its elements as required. ☐

STEP
10
Adding data
to an existing
chart

Very commonly we spend some time formatting a beautiful graph, only to realize that some additional data need to be displayed. In fact, your boss just called: he tells you that the snowfall, maximum and minimum temperature data must be included in the same graph.

a. Right Click on your chart → Select Data... → Add → go to the Series name box and select cell F4, then replace whatever is on the Series Value with the Maximum temperature [°C] (Maximum temperature [°F]) cells (F5:F16) → OK. ☐

b. Do the same to add the Minimum temperature data [°C] (Minimum temperature data [°F]) to the graph, and Click OK in the Select Data Source box. ☐

c. Make your maximum temperature line red, your mean temperature line purple and your minimum temperature line a light blue that contrasts enough with the precipitation columns. ☐

d. Add the snowfall data in the graph so that they appear as a stacked column on top of the precipitation columns, and pick a color for the snowfall columns that goes well with the graph. ☐

e. Do whatever you need to do so that both snowfall and rainfall legends are together in the legend box, and that the mean temperature legend appears between the maximum and minimum temperature legends. ☐

f. Reduce the gap size between precipitation columns to 60%. ☐

STEP
11
Modifying axis
scales

There is only one thing still bothering us from our climatic graph: the Precipitation [mm] (Precipitation [in]) and Temperature [°C] (Temperature [°F]) axis scales do not match with the major gridlines (which derive from the Precipitation [mm] (Precipitation [in]) axis). Just add major gridlines to the temperature scale to see the problem. We could just delete the gridlines, or force them to match. Let's do the latter: the only way is to make sure we have the same number of axis ticks, and for now we have 10 (8) ticks for the Temperature

[°C] (Temperature [°F]) axis and only 9 (7) for the Precipitation [mm] (Precipitation [in]) axis. It is therefore easier to add one to the Precipitation [mm] (Precipitation [in]) scale.

a. If you are working with metric units, **Right Click** on the primary *y-axis* (Precipitation [mm]) and in the **Maximum** box type **90** and press **Enter**. If you are using Imperial units, **Right Click** on the primary *y-axis* (Precipitation [in]) and in the **Maximum** box type **4** and press **Enter**. Problem solved! Your chart is finished and should look like this (screenshot for Imperial units not shown):

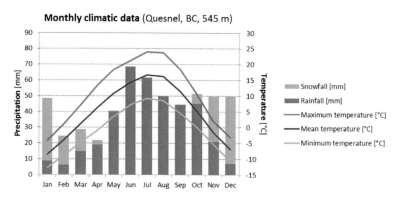

STEP
12
Black & white
or gray scale
charts

Many times we do not have a color printer and even if we do, people will lose the colorful beauty by photocopying our charts. It is therefore a good idea to produce nice graphs that do not depend on color to be understood. Let's apply that principle to our climatic chart then.

a. Create a duplicate of your color graph, which we will now edit.

b. Make the Snowfall [mm] (Snowfall [in]) columns light gray and the Rainfall [mm] (Rainfall [in]) columns darker gray.

c. **Right Click** on the Maximum temperature [°C] (Maximum temperature [°F]) line and make it plain black with a 1.5 pt width; do the same for the Mean temperature [°C] (Mean temperature [°F]) and Minimum temperature [°C] (Minimum temperature [°F]) data lines (they will all look the same after this procedure, but wait...).

d. **Right Click** on the Maximum temperature [°C] (Maximum temperature [°F]) data line → **Format Data Series...** → **Marker Options** → **Built-in** → choose the triangle size **7** and make it black (**Marker Fill** → **Solid fill**, then **Marker Line Color** → **No line**).

e. Repeat the same procedure for Mean temperature [°C] (Mean temperature [°F]) and Minimum temperature [°C] (Minimum temperature [°F]) data lines but choose a square and circle as markers, respectively, both size **5** and entirely black. All done! Your chart should look like this (screenshot for Imperial units not shown):

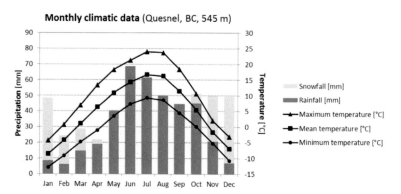

One of the major improvements of Excel® 2016 was the introduction of new chart types, some of them missed by statisticians before. I personally had to use a different software for my PhD thesis just because Excel could not handle a box & whisker graph. Let's just quickly explore these options, only if you have Excel® 2016.

a. While you are in the COMPOUND CHARTS sheet and with the cursor anywhere inside the data table, go to the Insert tab and Click on the lower right corner arrow of the Charts box (called See All Charts). Then go to the All Charts box and explore the following options by looking at the preview: Treemap, Sunburst, Histogram, Box & Whisker, Waterfall and Funnel. These are the brand-new chart types (not all may be available in your specific Excel® 2016 version). Obviously they are not appropriate for our monthly climatic data, but let's not spend more time on chart types in detail because you are already an expert in the topic. Just keep in mind that Excel now has many more chart types.

b. Go to the MAP CHARTS sheet and using the Insert Map Chart (if available) produce a map of your own showing data that you find interesting. Mine is this:

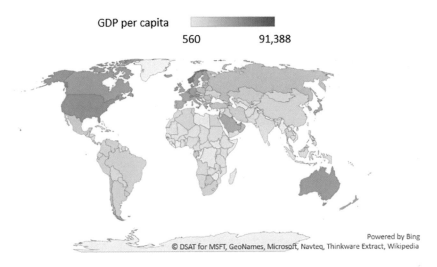

Buttons used in this step: Insert Map Chart

We are done with **Part A**!

STEP
13
Other new Excel 2016 charts (optional)

Part B - Applied exercise

In every example so far, this book told you what type of chart to produce for a specific purpose. In **Part B** you explore a very short example (**Figure 17**) so you decide what is the best chart type to tell the story you want to tell.

STEP
01
Creating the
chart you need!

a. Open the **chapter_05_part_B_ applied_exercise.xlsx** and save it in a safe location as **chapter_05_ part_B_applied_exercise_solved. xlsx**; use the **chapter_05_part_B_ applied_exercise_imperial.xlsx** file if you wish to work with acres instead of hectares. The database

Figure 17. In this short exercise you are the manager of forest land and to prevent fires like this one, you need to classify different areas according to fire risk; most importantly, you need to visualize the data as a beautiful chart.

looks familiar to you because it contains a list of your forest stands from **Chapter 4**, their fire risk classification and their area in hectares or acres (for Imperial users).

b. Use formulas in cells G5:G8 to calculate the total surface, in hectares or acres, for each of the fire risk categories.

c. Create a chart, of the type that you chose, that shows the total area of fire risk categories and their equivalent percentages. Be creative and make sure the color scheme is appropriate to tell this story (it's about fire!), that it has titles, units, and any additional information that you think will make the graph worth being on the cover of a National Geographic magazine. You may refer to **Section 5** below to consider all the good practices when creating charts.

5. Summary of good practices when creating charts

Whenever you need to create a chart, from now on, consider these very useful principles, and look at the appendix below to clearly understand what they mean:

- **Demolish ugly defaults**. The Excel defaults always need improvement; you need to edit your charts 100% of the time; never leave a chart as is; not enhancing default charts is strictly forbidden. I cannot make it any clearer...
- **Apply spatial harmony**. Always make sure chart elements (legends, equations, titles, axis titles, etc.) are harmoniously and aesthetically distributed in the space available.
- **Tell a story**. Charts tell a story and convey a message: make sure the chart type that you choose and its color scheme help you tell that story.
- **Empower completeness**. Always make sure all your axes are labeled, your units are included, the legend is clear, etc., so that your chart is as self-explanatory as possible; avoid unnecessary abbreviations.
- **Consider gray scales**. We all love color, but remember that we mostly print in black and white; it is always a good idea to create charts where you will distinguish elements even if they are printed in a gray scale.
- **Passionately love appropriate scales**. Always check that your scales are appropriate, with a reasonable number of tick marks (not too many, not too few) and avoiding unnecessary decimal places.

Appendix - Default vs. personalized graphs

See the difference in the charts when you spend a little bit of time fixing them. The left column shows a default graph, and the right is your personalized chart.

Before

After

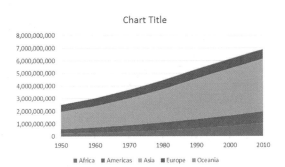

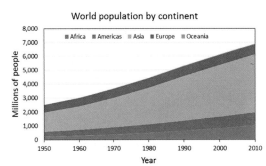

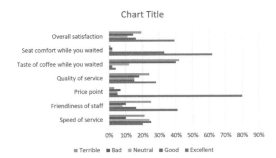

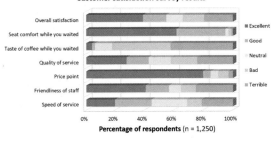

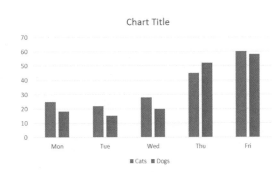

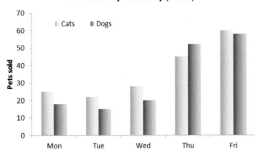

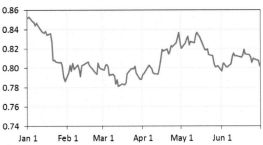

Before

Number of owners

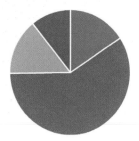

■ Ford   ■ Toyota   ■ Mazda   ■ Other

Height [m]

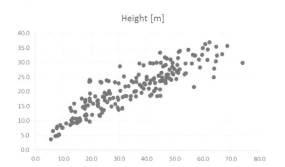

Chart Title

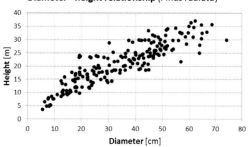

After

Preferred car brands

Diameter - height relationship (*Pinus radiata*)

CO₂ emissions, GDP and infant mortality

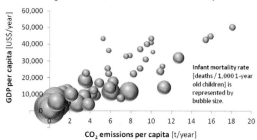

CHAPTER 6

Pivot tables and charts

1. Introduction and learning objectives

I could write a poem about how useful, versatile, magical and beautiful *pivot tables* and pivot charts are, but this book is about your hands-on experience. I cannot wait for you to start with the procedures in this chapter since they involve probably the most revolutionary and time-saving of all Excel techniques. In **Part A** you will learn the basic functioning of pivot tables and charts while **Part B** is about applying them to a practical example. In both parts we will use data you are already familiar with, now demonstrating how to produce reports without typing a single formula.

The learning objectives are:

1. Understand the database structure required to produce pivot tables and pivot charts.
2. Create and edit pivot tables and charts.
3. Understand the flexibility of pivot tables and charts.
4. Understand how pivot tables and charts are dynamically linked to the source data.
5. Apply a variety of pivot table formats.

2. Specific skills

1. **Using pivot tables:** creating, editing, modifying and updating pivot tables.
2. **Choosing what to display in a pivot table:** filtering and sorting, collapsing and expanding.
3. **Changing the mathematical operations** performed by a pivot table.
4. **Choosing the best layout** for a pivot table.
5. **Changing the style** of a pivot table.
6. **Duplicating existing pivot tables** to save time.
7. **Grouping data** in pivot tables.
8. **Creating pivot charts** from pivot tables.
9. **Changing the data source** of a pivot table and chart.
10. **Introducing calculated fields** in pivot tables.

3. Background

3.1 Pivot tables

Almost every task we accomplish as students, professionals, business owners and decent individuals requires the collection, organization and analysis of data. In other words, you need to produce a solid database —be it to record your daily sales or track your weight loss— and then find a proper way of summarizing the information into something useful —sales per employee and retail location or kilograms lost per week. Simplifying this even more, you need a functional centralized *database* to produce convenient *reports*. What happens if you change or update your database? In the 21st Century, the report should automatically change with it. *Pivot tables* are the automatic reports in this parade, one of Excel's most fantastic features, and the reason why non-computer geeks or inexperienced programmers like you and I can go around the world with a smile not needing to learn hard-core programming. Trust me, you will LOVE pivot tables with all your heart. And if you are ever told they are complicated, don't believe it.

3.2 Pivot charts

A *pivot chart* is nothing more than the graphical representation of a pivot table, to which it is inevitably connected. Pivot charts can be of the same type as regular charts (bar, column, pie, etc.), so working with them will be easy for you. Enough *blah blah*, just go straight to the procedures!

4. Procedures

Through the following steps, you will complete all tasks described in **Section 2**, but not necessarily in the same order. Remember our legend convention as you read: **file name**, Excel location (tab, menu, button, dialog box, control, option or cell coordinates), keyboard or mouse button(s), **formula**, typed data and procedure.

Part A - Basic pivot table and chart functions

In this first part you will learn the basics of how pivot tables and pivot charts work or, to be fair, how they perform miracles.

STEP
01
Understanding database structure

a. Open the file **chapter_06_part_A_pivot_tables_charts.xlsx** and save it in a safe location as **chapter_06_part_A_pivot_tables_charts_solved.xlsx**. ☐

b. Go to the DATA sheet and analyze the database you have there. Well, it is the same database that you used ☐

Figure 18. These brave telemarketing sales associates who must deal with angry customers, making one sale every 10,000 calls, are paid by commission. The payroll manager does not know any Excel formulas but uses pivot tables at the end of the month to see exactly how much they earned. It takes him 2 seconds to do so.

in **Chapter 3**, showing the results you got through formulas in column K. In **Chapter 3** you generated some useful calculations like *commissions for Ryan in 2013, total sales by Martin*, etc. You needed the **=SUMIF( )** to get those numbers, and it took some time to generate them one by one. What if there was an automatic way of creating tables that show all the relevant information, with a flexible structure and formatting? For example, through the Historic sales by invoice database, you could immediately answer questions like:

1. What were the total sales and number of transactions per year?
2. What is the day in the week with the highest sales?
3. How are commissions distributed among employees, in different years?
4. What is the percentage of sales by payment method and what are the monthly commissions that you need to pay to Visa, Mastercard and Amex?
5. What is the total volume of sales of invoices from $0 to $5,000, from $5,000 to $10,000, and so on?

c. Believe it or not, today you will learn how to answer these questions automatically with just a few mouse clicks and without using a single formula. Let's begin. ☐

d. Find our ***Best Practices*** rule #6 and make sense of it as you complete this chapter. ☐

e. Select columns K and L and delete them; we only included them as a reminder of what is about to become a thing of the past. Pivot tables are the future! ☐

Let's answer **Question 1** above: *What were the total sales and number of transactions per year?*

STEP
02
Creating your
first pivot table

a. In the DATA sheet, select all records (B4:I1555), then go to Insert → PivotTable → OK. ☐

b. From the PivotTable Fields menu that appears on the right, select Year with the mouse and drag it to the Rows quadrant below. ☐

c. Now move the Total [$] field to the Values quadrant. Have you seen the magic that just happened? ☐

d. Label the sheet Q1 and move it so that it appears after the DATA sheet. ☐

e. Select column B in your Q1 sheet and format numbers to appear with thousand separators and no decimals, and remove the gridlines if you wish (they personally annoy me so much!). ☐

Buttons used in this step: PivotTable

STEP
03
Filtering and
formatting

a. While in your Q1 sheet, let's see how you can display whatever you want in the pivot table. Assume you are not interested in displaying years 2011 and 2015 as they are both incomplete; Click on the arrow button of the Row Labels cell (which may be in cell A3), and simply unclick 2011 and 2015, then Click OK. ☐

b. While your cursor is placed in the pivot table, the PivotTable Tools appear as a new tab. Go to the Design tab and choose a PivotTable Style that you like. ☐

c. Make years 2011 and 2015 appear again. ☐

STEP
04
Duplicating
pivot tables
and changing
operation

In the example above, we summarized the total sales by summing the values. Now you are interested in knowing how many invoices were created each day, and what the average sale per invoice was. Instead of creating a new pivot table from scratch and formatting it again, we will just copy-paste the existing one and apply any changes afterwards:

a. Select your entire pivot table (should be cells A3:B9), press Ctrl+C, go to cell E3 and press Ctrl+V; and immediately auto-adjust the width of the columns of your new table. ☐

b. Now we want to count the invoices, so Right Click on the Sum of Total [$] cell (F3) → Value Field Settings... and choose Count from the list, then OK. Boom! So easy! Wow, a total of 1,551 invoices for all the years displayed. From 2011 to 2014 you see a consistent growth in your business both through total sales and number of transactions. ☐

c. Now copy-paste a third table in cell I3 and calculate the average invoice value. ☐

STEP
05
Updating a
pivot table, and
changing its
data source

One of the beautiful features of a pivot table is that it changes dynamically as you alter the data source, although you need to manually update a pivot table to reflect those changes. Let's see:

a. Go to your DATA sheet and insert a line between rows 7 and 8 (someone forgot to input a large invoice); copy the formulas from cells D7, G7 and H7 to cells D8, G8 and D8, respectively, and fill the remaining records with the following data for each cell: 0004 (B8), 2011-11-18 (C8), Mastercard (E8), 251500, (F8) and Martin (I8).

b. Go to your Q1 sheet and put the cursor anywhere within your first table (summing the invoices), then Right Click → Refresh. You should see the total for 2011 increase to 336,649 (before it was 54,969). This worked because you entered a value in the middle of the pivot table data source.

c. Refresh your other two tables in the Q1 sheet.

d. Go to your DATA sheet and in the bottom of the data range select cells B1556:I1556 and simply copy them with the mouse to create a new line at the end, leaving the values as they are from the automatic pasting (invoice in line 1557 should be 1553, date 2015-04-27, and so on).

e. Just change the value in cell F1557 of your DATA sheet to 200000 (we are using big numbers so that it is easy to visualize the changes in the pivot tables).

f. Refresh your first pivot table in sheet Q1 again and you will notice nothing changed; this is because the source data were set up to go up to row 1556 of your DATA sheet.

g. Go to your first pivot table of sheet Q1 and Click on the Change Data Source button under the PivotTable Tools → Analyze tab, then simply change the range in the Table/Range box to include row 1557, then Click OK and see how your table now updated automatically, increasing the total 2015 sales to 672,352.

h. Change the data source to include line 1557 in your other two pivot tables in the Q1 sheet.

Buttons used in this step: Change Data Source

You have easily mastered the basics of pivot tables. Your Q1 sheet should look like this (with your own color style):

	A	B	C	D	E	F	G	H	I	J
1										
2										
3	Row Labels ▾	Sum of Total [$]			Row Labels ▾	Count of Total [$]			Row Labels ▾	Average of Total [$]
4	2011	336,649			2011	10			2011	33,665
5	2012	1,090,197			2012	238			2012	4,581
6	2013	1,288,280			2013	453			2013	2,844
7	2014	2,121,095			2014	694			2014	3,056
8	2015	672,352			2015	158			2015	4,255
9	Grand Total	5,508,572			Grand Total	1,553			Grand Total	3,547
10										
11										

Now let's answer **Question 2** above, which says: *what is the day in the week with the highest sales?*

STEP
06
Conditional
formatting and
sorting

a. Go to your DATA sheet and insert a new column between columns D and E, write Weekday on the field header (E4) and fill the data with a formula that, based on the Date column, displays the weekday in *ddd* format (e.g. Mon, Tue, etc.). Hint: you may use a formula that incorporates **=TEXT( )** and **=WEEKDAY( )**, or just **=WEEKDAY( )** with a specific formatting display (check **Chapter 2** or the corresponding answer key file).

b. Create a pivot table in a new sheet labeled Q2, which sums the total sales by weekday, displaying the weekdays in the rows of the pivot table (interesting statistic since it will help you determine your staff requirements). If for some reason the Weekday field does not appear in the list as you create the pivot table, just refresh it.

c. Format the total sales data of your new table to display no decimals and a thousand separator. Hide the gridlines if you wish.

d. Add Conditional Formatting in the Sum of Total [$] column displaying Data Bars with a Gradient Fill color of your choice. ☐

e. Did you notice how Excel recognizes that we are using weekdays and sorts them in chronological order in your Row Labels column of your Q2 pivot table? How nice! However, we now want to arrange the days from highest to lowest total sales; as you would do for any table, locate your cursor within any cell with data in your column B, and apply sorting in descending order. Friday is by far the most productive day, followed by Tuesday and Monday. Sunday is at the bottom because that day is full of browsers that don't buy anything except for ice cream somewhere else. ☐

STEP
07
Adding a filter
report and
some editing

You wonder if Friday is consistently the day with the largest total sales among all sales associates. Maybe Ana sells better on Wednesdays! Just imagine all the formulas you would need to use to answer these questions were it not for the magic and simplicity of pivot tables. Here we go:

a. While your cursor is in your pivot table of the Q2 sheet, drag the Sold by field in the PivotTable Fields list to the Filters quadrant below, and notice how you now have another option to choose from in cell B1. ☐

b. Apply the filter in cell B1 and, one at a time, choose Ana, Darya, Maria, Martin and Ryan to make comparisons. Indeed, the most productive day does vary among employees. Notice how Excel automatically keeps the sorting that you defined for the pivot table. With the filter option, however, you can only view one employee at a time, so now let's create another pivot table that permanently shows all five people: ☐

c. In cell B1, remove the filter by applying the (All) option again. ☐

d. Copy and paste your pivot table of rows A1:B11 to cell D1. ☐

e. Place the cursor over your second pivot table and with the mouse, drag the Sold by field from the Filters quadrant to the Columns quadrant. ☐

f. Now that the Filters option is empty in this new table, let's add the Year field to the Filters quadrant, and choose to show 2014 results only. ☐

g. Go to cell D4 and type Weekday, then type Sold by in cell E3, and auto-adjust the column widths of your new pivot table. ☐

STEP
08
Your first pivot
chart

a. While your cursor is over your second pivot table of sheet Q2, the one you just created, go to PivotTable Tools → Analyze tab and Click on PivotChart and select the 3-D Stacked Column option. ☐

b. Add a light gray border: Right Click on the plot area of the chart → Format Walls... and then delete the overall chart border. ☐

c. From your pivot chart, change the Year field to display 2013 only, and see how your pivot table linked to this chart also changed (both table and chart are innately connected). ☐

d. Now change the filter in cell E1 to display all years and see how your pivot chart changed too. ☐

e. Oops! There were mistakes in your DATA sheet! Both cells G1557 and G8 had two extra zeros! Their values should be 2000 and 2515, respectively. Fix that and then refresh your pivot tables in the Q2 sheet. ☐

f. It turns out Ryan will be leaving the company soon; he was so good that it will be painful to remember him, so from your pivot chart in the Sold by drop-down menu unclick the name of this fine young man. You now get the idea of how flexible pivot tables and charts are. ☐

Buttons used in this step: Pivot Chart

You have easily mastered the basics of pivot tables and charts. Your Q2 sheet should look like this (if you don't have the data bars in the tables, it means you skipped the conditional formatting procedure in **Step 6** above):

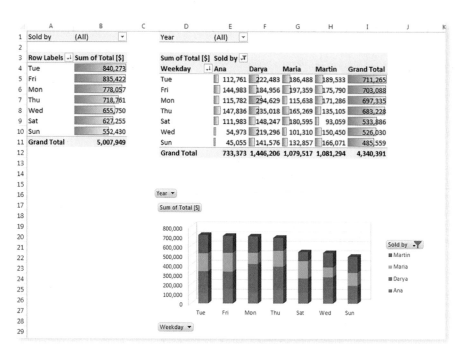

STEP

09

More display
options

a. Now we will answer the very interesting **Question 3**: *How are commissions distributed among employees, in different years?*

b. In the DATA sheet, insert a column between columns I and J with a header called Commission [$] in cell J4 and fill its cells with a formula that multiplies the Amount [$] in column G by 0.025 (2.5% commission, the industry standard).

c. On your own, create a pivot table to be displayed in a new sheet labeled Q3, to the right of Q2, which shows employee names in rows, years in columns and sum of commissions inside.

d. Properly format the table in terms of decimals and general appearance following your criteria.

e. This table that you just created displays names in rows and years in columns; let's explore another option: select your table (cells A3:G10) and duplicate it by copying-pasting it in cell J3.

f. Using the PivotTable Fields menu on the right, drag the Year field from the Columns to the Rows quadrant.

g. Click on the [-] buttons to the left of your employee names and see how you can expand and collapse them to show years or not; leave them all expanded except for Darya and Maria. Isn't this FANTASTIC? Can you believe that you have lived all these years without pivot tables? Your life will never be the same again.

Your Q3 sheet should look like this:

	A	B	C	D	E	F	G	H	I	J	K	L
1												
2												
3	Sum of Commission [$]	Column Labels								Row Labels	Sum of Commission [$]	
4	Row Labels	2011	2012	2013	2014	2015	Grand Total			⊞Ana	16,369.94	
5	Ana	52.42	3,801.37	4,043.87	6,703.44	1,768.84	16,369.94			⊟Darya	32,281.38	
6	Darya	52.20	8,233.19	7,791.55	14,174.36	2,030.08	32,281.38			2011	52.20	
7	Maria	191.93	6,384.94	6,576.18	8,764.51	2,178.81	24,096.37			2012	8,233.19	
8	Martin	560.01	3,799.22	5,923.79	11,146.34	2,706.67	24,136.03			2013	7,791.55	
9	Ryan	433.30	2,116.02	4,420.87	6,557.21	1,373.46	14,900.86			2014	14,174.36	
10	Grand Total	1,289.86	24,334.74	28,756.25	47,345.87	10,057.86	111,784.58			2015	2,030.08	
11										⊟Maria	24,096.37	
12										2011	191.93	
13										2012	6,384.94	
14										2013	6,576.18	
15										2014	8,764.51	
16										2015	2,178.81	
17										⊞Martin	24,136.03	
18										⊞Ryan	14,900.86	
19										Grand Total	111,784.58	

STEP
10

Displaying values
as percentages,
grouping fields
and minor edits

It's **Question 4**'s turn: *What is the percentage of sales by payment method and what are the monthly commissions that you need to pay to Visa, Mastercard and Amex?*

a. Select all your data in the DATA sheet and create a new pivot table in a new sheet to be labeled Q4 (remember to put your sheets in order within your file). ☐

b. Add the Method field to the Rows quadrant and the Total [$] field to the Values quadrant (format those numbers immediately please!). ☐

c. Remove the dash (-) category that displays 0.00 sales from the pivot table (those were cancelled invoices). ☐

d. You want to know the percentage of sales by payment method, so add the Total [$] field to the Values quadrant again and in this new column (which should be in column C), Right Click on any cell → Show Values As → % of Grand Total. ☐

e. Overwrite cell C3 with %, show only one decimal for those percentages, align them to the center and auto-adjust the width of column C. ☐

f. Now let's learn to move fields in your pivot table; for some reason you want the percentages displayed before the sum, so simply select cells C3:C12 and, with the mouse, move them so that they appear immediately after the Row Labels column. ☐

g. Sort the table contents by highest to lowest percentage of sales, so that Visa appears first and Transfer last. ☐

h. We have only partially answered **Question 4**, so let's complete this. Go to your DATA sheet and add a column between I and J with a header called Credit card fee [$], and fill the cells with a formula that uses =IF( ) to multiply the Total [$] values by 0.015 if the invoice is paid by Visa, Mastercard or Amex, and displays a dash for all other types. Hint: use =OR( ) in the logical test (first argument) of =IF( ). ☐

i. Go back to your Q4 sheet, copy your first table (cells A3:C12) to cell F3, and auto-adjust its column widths. Refresh this table and edit the Row labels so that only Visa, Mastercard and Amex appear. ☐

j. Remove both the % and Total [$] fields from the Values quadrant and instead add the Credit card fee [$] field to the Values quadrant (make sure this field is set up to be summed and not counted). ☐

k. Move the Method field to the Columns quadrant. ☐

l. Add the Year field to the Rows quadrant and then also the Date field to the Rows quadrant, below the Year field. Don't panic! We are not done yet. ☐

m. Right Click on any of the dates within your pivot table (e.g. cell F9), then select Group... and select Months from the By box list, and Click OK. Wow!!! Excel detects that we are using dates in the field and then automatically allows us to group them in any desired interval. What was done by you in one second with Excel took hours or days only a few decades ago, all by hand in wrinkled coffee-spilled paper handbooks. Good times to live on Earth, as instead of executing endless manual calculations we can spend more time living our lives. ☐

n. Collapse years 2011 and 2012 so that you see the entire table, then type Card fees [$] in cell F3, Card in cell G3 and Year in cell F4. Finally, auto-adjust the column widths. Well, the credit card companies have commissioned a total of 55,119 from your sales since you started the business. ☐

ProTip

If your spreadsheet masterpiece will be used by multiple users, make it error-proof via data validation and selective cell & workbook protection. **Chapter 7** will show you how!

The top of your Q4 sheet should look like this:

	A	B	C	D	E	F	G	H	I	J	K
1											
2											
3	Row Labels ⬆⬇	%	Sum of Total [$]			Card fees [$]	Card ⬇				
4	Visa	59.1%	2,959,080			Year	⬇ Amex	Mastercard	Visa	Grand Total	
5	Cheque	16.7%	834,030			⊞2011	95	264	507	867	
6	Mastercard	13.3%	666,061			⊞2012	425	1,030	9,578	11,033	
7	Debit	4.4%	219,651			⊟2013	38	2,506	11,362	13,905	
8	Cash	4.2%	208,245			Jan		58	726	784	
9	Amex	1.0%	49,490			Feb	2	304	377	684	
10	Transfer	0.9%	47,274			Mar		56	1,161	1,217	
11	Gift card	0.5%	24,117			Apr	1	111	1,436	1,548	
12	Grand Total	100.0%	5,007,949			May		109	283	391	
13						Jun		340	992	1,333	
14						Jul	30	176	541	748	
15						Aug	4	58	1,153	1,215	
16						Sep		479	2,359	2,838	
17						Oct		236	1,133	1,369	
18						Nov		548	164	712	
19						Dec		29	1,037	1,066	
20						⊟2014	137	5,528	18,820	24,485	
21						Jan	17	932	1,080	2,029	
22						Feb	2	406	1,425	1,833	
23						Mar	48	168	1,716	1,932	
24						Apr		922	992	1,914	
25						May	1	677	2,034	2,712	
26						Jun		211	1,606	1,817	

STEP

11

More grouping!

Finally, **Question 5**: *What is the total volume of sales of invoices from $0 to $5,000, from $5,000 to $10,000, and so on?*

a. Select all your data in the DATA sheet and create a new pivot table in a new sheet to be labeled Q5 (remember to put your sheets in order within your file). ☐

b. Add the Total [$] field to the Rows quadrant, then Right Click on any of the values and select Group..., then type 0 in the Starting at box and 5000 in the By box (leave the other one alone), and Click OK (note: negative numbers are returns and we do not want to display those). ☐

c. Add the Total [$] field but this time to the Values quadrant and, if necessary, change the operation to Sum with the Value Field Settings... button. ☐

d. Format the values to display no decimals and thousand separators and remove the <0 category from the Row Labels list. Clearly, the largest portion of your sales comes from invoices of less than $10,000. What is this company selling, by the way? It appears to be billing strongly but we don't know the operation costs. ☐

e. Add another column to the pivot table that gets the percentage of each sales range with respect to the grand total; change the header of that new column to % (centered) as you did before, and show only one decimal for those percentages. ☐

We are done with **Part A**. Even though time flies when you are experiencing the magic of Excel, the good news is that **Part B** is very short! Your Q5 sheet should be:

	A	B	C	D
1				
2				
3	Row Labels ⬇	Sum of Total [$]	%	
4	0-5000	1,432,918	28.6%	
5	5000-10000	1,414,819	28.2%	
6	10000-15000	753,369	15.0%	
7	15000-20000	431,950	8.6%	
8	20000-25000	342,398	6.8%	
9	25000-30000	269,704	5.4%	
10	30000-35000	133,808	2.7%	
11	35000-40000	78,977	1.6%	
12	40000-45000	88,473	1.8%	
13	70000-75000	70,581	1.4%	
14	Grand Total	5,016,997	100.0%	

Part B - Applying pivot tables and charts to your data (inventory hours)

Now we can go back to exercises you already completed and move forward in analyzing the data by applying pivot tables and charts.

Figure 19. A reminder that installing traffic lights involves dangers such as electrocution or falling from the heights; your crews need to be paid promptly and this is possible thanks to pivot tables.

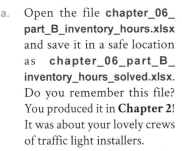

STEP 01
Open, save and immediate pivot table

a. Open the file **chapter_06_part_B_inventory_hours.xlsx** and save it in a safe location as **chapter_06_part_B_inventory_hours_solved.xlsx**. Do you remember this file? You produced it in **Chapter 2**! It was about your lovely crews of traffic light installers. ☐

b. Create a pivot table from the INVENTORY HOURS sheet in a new sheet to be labeled CREW SUMMARY that shows the Total hours, Payment [$] and Lights installed by each crew (with crews in the Row Labels). ☐

STEP 02
Custom field based on calculations

Do you remember spending much more time using formulas to get the same data in **Chapter 2**? Now, remember that the Payment [$] field in the table considered payment per person, and each crew had two people. We will add a field in the pivot table that calculates the total amount of money to be paid by the company considering the two workers per crew.

a. While your cursor is anywhere in the pivot table you created in the previous step, go to the PivotTable Tools tab → Analyze → Field, Items & Sets button → Calculated Field... → Double Click on Payment [$] within the Fields list below, and then type *2 in the Formula Bar, so that the formula that appears there is ='Payment [$]'*2; then Click OK. ☐

b. Move this new custom field so that it appears to the right of the Sum of Payment [$] column. ☐

c. Hide the gridlines, add an entire column to the left of your pivot table, an additional row above it, and type Crew summary in cell B2 (font size 14, **bold**). ☐

d. Edit the headers in row 4 so that they appear in the following order and are called Crew #, Total time [h], Payment [$/person], Payment [$/crew] and No. of lights, auto-adjust the width of your columns and center everything in your table. ☐

e. Format the numbers in your table so that any dollar values appear with two decimals and thousand separators, while hours and number of lights should show no decimals. ☐

Buttons used in this step: Field Items & Sets

Your table in the CREW SUMMARY sheet should look like this:

Crew # ▾	Total time [h]	Payment [$/person]	Payment [$/crew]	No. of lights
1	190	3,907.25	7,814.50	77
2	178	3,618.75	7,237.50	72
3	166	3,280.00	6,560.00	68
Grand Total	533	10,806.00	21,612.00	217

STEP

03

You are an
expert on pivot
tables now!

a.　Create a pivot table from the INVENTORY HOURS sheet in a new sheet to be labeled MONTHLY SUMMARY. ☐

b.　Add the Date field in the Rows quadrant of the pivot table and then add to the Values quadrant the Total hours field, Payment [$] and a custom field that multiplies the Payment [$] by 2, just as you did in the previous step. ☐

c.　Group the Date values by month. ☐

d.　Add the Crew field to the Rows quadrant, below Date. ☐

e.　Edit the headers so that they appear in the following order and are called Total time [h], Payment [$/person] and Payment [$/crew], and auto-adjust the width of your columns. ☐

f.　Hide the gridlines, add a column to the left of your pivot table, an additional row above it, and type Monthly summary in cell B2 (font size 14, **bold**). ☐

Your table in the MONTHLY SUMMARY sheet should look like this:

Monthly summary

Row Labels	Total time [h]	Payment [$/person]	Payment [$/crew]
⊟ Apr	123	2,503.75	5,007.50
1	47	952.50	1,905.00
2	43	871.25	1,742.50
3	34	680.00	1,360.00
⊟ May	99	2,061.25	4,122.50
1	30	691.25	1,382.50
2	25	507.50	1,015.00
3	45	862.50	1,725.00
⊟ Jun	96	2,023.50	4,047.00
1	17	360.00	720.00
2	59	1,256.00	2,512.00
3	21	407.50	815.00
⊟ Jul	95	1,911.00	3,822.00
1	50	1,057.50	2,115.00
2	30	531.00	1,062.00
3	15	322.50	645.00
⊟ Aug	80	1,556.50	3,113.00
1	25	441.00	882.00
2	15	318.00	636.00
3	41	797.50	1,595.00
⊟ Sep	41	750.00	1,500.00
1	23	405.00	810.00
2	8	135.00	270.00
3	11	210.00	420.00
Grand Total	533	10,806.00	21,612.00

Now it is time to look at some very useful, extremely simple techniques to make your spreadsheets error-proof, functional and secure in **Chapter 7**. You are making great progress!

5. Review of functions used

=IF( )
=OR( )
=TEXT( )
=WEEKDAY( )

Error-proof files & other advanced features

1. Introduction and learning objectives

This chapter is about learning some more advanced but remarkably useful features of Excel; it will truly make you a genius Excel user if you comply with these learning objectives:

1. Learn the three techniques to produce secure and error-proof spreadsheet files: *data validation, cell protection* and *password protection.*
2. Understand and perform *What-if Analysis* with *Scenario Manager.*
3. Understand the use of *Goal Seek* and *Solver*
4. Understand the concept of *macros* and apply basic examples.
5. Merge all your Excel knowledge to produce an error-proof, functional spreadsheet application.

2. Specific skills

1. **Applying *data validation:*** understanding how to create, edit and delete data validation rules; creating special rules based on formulas; editing input and output data validation messages; identifying invalid data.
2. **Understanding the =INDIRECT( )** function.
3. **Applying a *dependent list*** data validation tool with drop-down menus.
4. **Understanding the *Scenario Manager*** tool and adding its shortcut to the *Quick Access Toolbar.*
5. **Applying the *Goal Seek* and *Solver*** tools and identifying typical examples where they are appropriate.
6. **Recording fixed reference *macros*** to automate a multi-step task.
7. **Recording relative reference *macros*** to automate a multi-step task for specific cells.
8. **Producing error-proof** spreadsheets with *data validation and cell protection.*
9. **Adding password protection** so that your Excel file cannot be opened by the enemy.

3. Background

3.1 Data validation and sheet protection

In order to make spreadsheets error-proof, *data validation* and *sheet protection* are excellent tools. **Data validation** consists of restricting what you can enter in specific cells, and is ideal to avoid errors when multiple users manipulate a workbook. Sheet protection allows you to simply block typing in certain cells, and is fantastic for protecting cells whose contents and formatting should not be overwritten.

3.2 What-If analysis

You will apply two options of *What-If* analysis with Excel:

1. **Manual *What-If analysis*:** plug in new values and observe the effects on formula cells (you have been doing this throughout this book!).
2. ***Scenario Manager*:** a tool that allows you to store pre-defined values to be entered in specific cells and use them as required.

3.3 What-If analysis in reverse: Goal Seek and Solver

Now consider the following examples where the *What-If* analysis goes backwards:

1. ***Goal Seek*:** tool that allows you to get the exact input value you require for a formula to produce the desired result.
2. ***Solver*:** a tool that allows you to define the multiple input values required to produce a desired outcome in a formula, given possible restrictions.

The Solver tool might not be installed by default; if this is the case, follow these steps: File → Options → Add-Ins, select Analysis ToolPak from the list → Go… → Click on the Solver Add-in box to turn it on → OK.

3.4 Macros

Macros are the door to more advanced programming, and are simply defined as a sequence of events automatically executed by Excel but previously defined and recorded by the user. You will learn this concept at the end of **Part A** of this chapter.

4. Procedures

Through the following steps, you will complete all tasks described in **Section 2**, but not necessarily in the same order. Remember our legend convention as you read: file name, Excel location (tab, menu, button, dialog box, control, option or cell coordinates), keyboard or mouse button(s), formula, typed data and procedure.

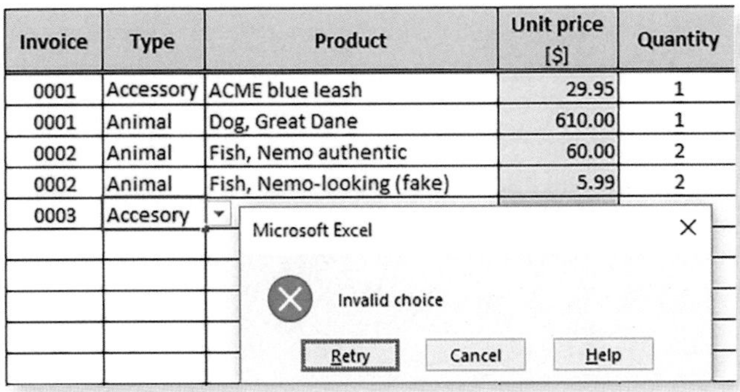

Invoice	Type	Product	Unit price [$]	Quantity
0001	Accessory	ACME blue leash	29.95	1
0001	Animal	Dog, Great Dane	610.00	1
0002	Animal	Fish, Nemo authentic	60.00	2
0002	Animal	Fish, Nemo-looking (fake)	5.99	2
0003	Accesory			

Microsoft Excel ✕

✕ Invalid choice

Retry   Cancel   Help

Figure 20. Do you have a lousy employee with terrible spelling, like this one typing "Accesory" with one "s"? Suffer no more. With data validation and other tricks now to be learned, this employee will be forced to type the right thing after receiving the "Invalid choice" message.

Part A - Data validation, What-If analysis and macros

Data validation

Data validation is a simple procedure specifying what can be entered in a cell or group; with constraints related to formatting (e.g. accept numbers formatted as dates only), ranges (e.g. input values between 0 and 50 only), or a specific list of pre-determined options. There are also custom validation options based on formulas giving almost unlimited power to control what goes in cells. The following steps will show, with basic examples, the types of data validation you can use. In **Part B** you will apply some of them in a real example, together with cell protection, to produce an absolutely error-proof spreadsheet.

STEP
01
Whole numbers

a. Open the file **chapter_07_part_A_advanced_features.xlsx** and save it in a safe location as **chapter_07_part_A_advanced_features_solved.xlsx**; if you wish to work with Imperial units, use the file **chapter_07_part_A_advanced_features_imperial.xlsx**. In the blank cells for each example of the DATA VALIDATION sheet we will only allow entries that meet the specified conditions. Let's begin: ☐

b. Select cells C8:C10, then go to Data → Data Validation → select Whole number in the Allow list, and type 30 in the Minimum box and 50 in the Maximum box (notice that you could use cell references for that), then Click OK. ☐

c. Manually fill cells C8, C9 and C10 deliberately violating our validation rule to see what happens (e.g. enter a number larger than 50 or a text string). ☐

d. Manually fill the three cells with 38, 40 and 42, respectively, to comply with the validation rule. ☐

Buttons used in this step: Data Validation ☑⊘

STEP
02
Only positive numbers

a. Select cells F8:F10, go to the Data → Data Validation button (you might want to add it to the Quick Access Toolbar) and in the Allow list select Decimal, then choose greater than or equal to in the Data box, and type 0 (zero) in the Minimum box; before clicking OK go to the Error Alert tab and in the Error message box type Value must be a positive number, then Click OK. ☐

b. Try entering a negative value or text in cell F8 and see what happens. ☐

c. Enter these numbers in cells F8, F9 and F10, respectively: 10.5, 14.8 and 20.9. ☐

Buttons used in this step: Data Validation ☑⊘

It is typical that we cannot enter future dates in a database, and that may happen if someone just types the month and day since Excel might add the current year by default.

STEP
03
No future dates

a. Select cells I8:I10, Click on the Data Validation button (really, have you not put it in your Quick Access Toolbar yet?) and in the Allow list of the Settings tab select Date, then choose less than or equal to in the Data box, and in the End date box type =TODAY( ); go to the Error Alert tab and in the Error message box type Please enter a date not past the current date, then Click OK. ☐

b. Test if your validation restriction works in those cells, and then type these three dates into the cells: 2012-05-25; 1996-12-18 and 2008-05-21. ☐

Hopefully, as you have now added the Data Validation button in your Quick Access Toolbar, its image is no longer shown at the end of the steps below.

STEP
04
Times

a. Select cells L8:L10, Click on the Data Validation button and in the Allow list of the Settings tab select Time, then type 8:00 in the Start time box and 16:30 in the End time box; go to the Error Alert tab and in the Style list choose Warning and in the Error message box type You must enter a valid time within 8:00 and 16:30; are you sure your entry is correct?, then Click OK. By setting up a Warning instead of Stop we are more flexible with the data validation rule, allowing exceptions but notifying the user. ☐

b. Go to cell L8 and type 17:30, then see if your message appears and Click Yes; type 12:30 and 9:30 in the other two cells. ☐

STEP
05
Length of entries

a. Select cells O8:O10, Click on the Data Validation button and in the Allow list of the Settings tab select Text length, then choose less than or equal to in the Data box, and in the Maximum box type 4, then Click OK. ☐

b. See if your restriction works by typing a string longer than 4 characters, and after that fill the cells with ABCD, 1212 and ECU. ☐

STEP
06
Text only

In the previous example, you only restricted the length of the entry but it allowed both numbers and text strings. If you want to allow text only, we need a *custom* data validation rule based on a simple formula.

a. Select cells R8:R10, then Click on the Data Validation button and in the Allow list of the Settings tab select Custom, then type =ISTEXT(R8) in the Formula box, then go to the Error Alert tab and type These cells are for text strings only; no numbers please (leave Style in Stop mode), then Click OK. ☐

b. Make sure you are not allowed to enter numbers or logical statements in cells R8:R10 and then type Communism, is and nonsense respectively in cells R8, R9 and R10. ☐

STEP
07
Larger than previous

a. Select cells C18:C19 (yes, exclude cell C17), Click on the Data Validation button and in the Allow list of the Settings tab select Custom, then type =C18>C17 in the Formula box, and finally Click OK. ☐

b. Type 5 in cell C18 and see what happens, then Click Retry in the error message dialog and now type 20 in cell C18. ☐

c. Type 15 in cell C19, then fix it by typing 30. You are becoming an expert in *data validation*. ☐

STEP
08
Non-duplicates

a. Select cells F17:F19, Click on the Data Validation button and in the Allow list of the Settings tab select Custom then type =COUNTIF($F$17:$F$18,F17)=1 in the Formula box, and then Click OK. ☐

b. Type 20 in cell F17, then 20 again in cell F18, Click Retry when you see the error message and now type 21 in cell F18; finally enter 21 in cell F19. Oops! We made a mistake in the formula because we forgot to include cell F19 in the range, so it allowed the 21 to be duplicated. Leave the 21 in both cell F18 and F19. ☐

c. Select cells F17:F19 again, press the Data Validation button and change the formula to =COUNTIF($F$17:$F$19,F17)=1, then Click OK. You notice that since the 21 was already in cell F19, nothing happened when you fixed the formula because data validation only works for data entered after the rule was created (it also does not work when you copy-paste data in cells with validation rules). However, in a large database, you can check whether previously existent or pasted data complies with your new rules. ☐

d. Select cells F17:F19, go to Data → display the dropdown menu of Data Validation → Circle Invalid Data. Now you clearly see the problem (including cell L8 which we allowed to be 17:30). ☐

e. Type 22 in cell F19 and, if the circles disappeared automatically, make them appear again so that you see how cells F18 and F19 are no longer identified as invalid. ☐

f. Go to Data → Data Validation→ Clear Validation Circles. ☐

Buttons used in this step: Circle Invalid Data ⊞ Clear Validation circles ⊟

STEP 09
Begin with "a"

a. Select cells I17:I19, Click on Data Validation and in the Allow list of the Settings tab select Custom then type =LEFT(I17)="A" in the Formula box, and then Click OK. ☐

b. Try typing something that does not start with "A" to see how Excel gets mad at you once more (notice this is not case-sensitive). ☐

c. Type Andy flies in in cell I17, Airbus in cell I18, and A320 in cell I19. ☐

d. See what happens now when you Click on cell I17. ☐

STEP 10
Starting letter and string length

a. Select cells L17:L19, Click on Data Validation and in the Allow list of the Settings tab select Custom then type =COUNTIF(L17,"A????")=1 in the Formula box, and then Click OK. Only 5-character strings starting with "A" will be allowed. ☐

b. Try typing something violating our rule in cell L17. ☐

c. Type three different real English words that start with "a" and have five characters in cells L17, L18 and L19. ☐

STEP 11
Monday only

a. On your own, apply a data validation rule in cells O17:O19 that will only allow dates that correspond to Mondays (hint: the date format is already set up for you in those cells, so just concentrate on the Monday thing with a custom formula). ☐

b. Fill the cells with these dates which correspond to Mondays (if it did not let you use these, something is wrong with your data validation rule): 2014-03-17, 2014-03-10, 2014-02-24. ☐

STEP 12
Stay within budget

You are interested in entering cell values but without surpassing a total sum of those values, like when you decide what to spend your budget on.

a. Select cells R17:R19, Click on Data Validation and in the Allow list of the Settings tab select Custom then type =SUM($R$17:$R$19)<=500 in the Formula box (500 is our budget), and then Click OK. ☐

b. Type 150 in cell R17, 300 in cell R18 and 200 in cell R19... Oops! We are way above the budget! Click Retry and now enter 50 in cell R19. Do you see how flexible the custom validation rules are? Also, notice when to use relative references, like for **Step 10**, or fixed references like in this case. You must understand how those formulas work. ☐

STEP 13
Simple list

So far we have used formats and formulas to restrict what can go in a cell or not. However, you can also use a pre-determined list so that values are set up for a specific field. This is very useful when you don't want people typing with spelling errors or simply to use very specific categories (a principle that is fundamental to produce proper pivot tables). We will now only allow a specific list of countries to be entered in cells C27:C29.

a. Select cells C27:C29 and Click on the Data Validation button and in the Allow list of the Settings tab select List, then put the cursor in the Source box and go to the LISTS sheet and select cells B2:F2 (the Source box should show =LISTS!$B$2:$F$2), then Click OK. ☐

b. In your DATA VALIDATION sheet, go to cell C27 and see how now you can only choose between those five countries, and you even have a drop-down menu to select them (you can also type the country name but it should match any from the list). ☐

c. Fill cell C27 with Ecuador, cell C28 with Canada and cell C29 with Chile. ☐

What if you want to use lists as validation, but one list must appear only if a specific choice was made for another cell? For example, choose a country as in the previous step and in the next column see a drop-down menu of cities for that country only. This is exactly what we will do, but first we need to do some labeling for it to work.

a. Go to the LISTS sheet (where all the validation lists for this workbook are placed), select cells B3:B9 and label them Ecuador, then select cells C3:C9 and label them Canada; label cells D3:D9 as Chile, cells E3:E9 as Slovakia and cells F3:F9 as England (it is very important that you select exactly those cells and use exactly those labels). ☐

b. Go to the DATA VALIDATION sheet and select cells F27:F29 and Click on the Data Validation button and in the Allow list of the Settings tab select List, then put the cursor in the Source box, go to the LISTS sheet and select cells B2:F2 (the Source box should show =LISTS!$B$2:$F$2), then Click OK (yes, you are repeating this procedure from the previous step, but next comes the cool stuff). ☐

c. Go to the DATA VALIDATION sheet and select Slovakia for cell F27, England for cell F28 and Ecuador for cell F29. ☐

d. Select cells H27:H29 (these cells are merged with column I but it does not matter), then Click on Data Validation and in the Allow list of the Settings tab select List and type =INDIRECT(F27) in the Formula box (make sure the reference is NOT fixed), then Click OK. ☐

e. Understanding the =INDIRECT( ) function, one of my favorites, is important and very useful. This function simply tells Excel to treat a text string as a name. Let's take a little break from the data validation exercise to show you this: in your LISTS sheet, go to cell H3 and type =COUNTA(B2). Your result is 1 because this formula is counting the number of cells that are not empty in a range, in this case, just cell B2. Now overwrite this formula in cell H3 to be =COUNTA(INDIRECT(B2)). Your result is now 7 because =INDIRECT( ) is telling the =COUNTA( ) function to consider the contents of cell B2 as a name instead of a simple text string. Therefore, it is counting the number of non-empty cells in what you labeled with the name Ecuador (B3:B9). The =INDIRECT( ) function is incredibly useful when you need to copy formulas that can retrieve names when they are already written in a range of cells. You can now delete the contents of cell H3 and let's go back to data validation... ☐

f. In your DATA VALIDATION sheet, go to cell H27 and see how magically only Slovak cities appear as options for that cell; choose Bratislava (the capital) for cell H27, London for cell H28 and Quito for cell H29. Isn't this fantastic? ☐

g. Go to cell F28 and instead of England choose Canada; you see how this does not result in an error for now, but now go to cell H28 and make sure Canadian cities now appear in the drop-down menu; pick our lovely Vancouver, where this book was written. ☐

Scenario Manager

The Scenario Manager tool is fantastic and I will not waste your time trying to explain it. Simply follow the steps below and you will see.

a. Go to the SCENARIO MANAGER sheet and look at these data: we are estimating the profit resulting from selling three tropical fruits (cells C16:E16) based on two input variables: Harvesting cost [$/h] (cell C5) and Transport cost [$/ton/km] (Transport cost [$/ton/mi]) (cell C6). Just so you know, h stands for hours and ton refers to one metric ton (equivalent to 1,000 kg or 2,200 pounds). ☐

b. Play with different values in cells C5 and C6 and see their effect on the profits below (in this case, don't worry about returning to the original values in cells C5 or C6). What you are doing ☐

with this procedure is a manual *What-If analysis* that we referred to in **Section 3.2** above. It simply consists of changing input values to see the effect on output cells as the two are linked by formulas. You have done this a lot throughout this book so far. In the next procedures you will learn how to enhance this with the Scenario Manager approach.

c. Label cell C5 as harvest_cost and cell C6 as transport_cost (you will see why this is very useful when using scenarios). Now we will create three scenarios that store combinations of values for the Harvesting cost [$/h] and Transport cost [$/ton/km] (Transport cost [$/ton/mi]) that represent *best, most likely,* and *worst cases.*

d. Go to Data → What-If Analysis → Scenario Manager... → Add..., then type Best case in the Scenario name box, and while in the Changing cells box, select cells C5:C6 with the mouse; delete whatever appears in the Comment box and Click OK. In the Scenario Values dialog box, type 9.5 in the harvest_cost box and 4 in the transport_cost box (see why it was handy to label those cells?), then Click OK.

e. Repeat this procedure adding two more scenarios called Worst case (input 14.5 and 6.2 as the corresponding harvest and transport costs for that scenario) and Most likely (12 for harvest and 5.5 for transport).

f. Once you see the three scenarios you just created in the Scenario Manager dialog box, simply select any of them with the mouse and Click Show in the same box. See how the values in cells C5 and C6 automatically change to those stored by you for each scenario. You can close the Scenario Manager dialog box any time, and open it again by clicking on the What-If Analysis button → Scenario Manager... You can also edit the names and values for those scenarios any time.

g. You realize now that the Sales price values, in cells C13:E13, are typically subject to low, normal, and high seasons of retail sales. Label cells C13, D13 and E13 as price_passion, price_cocoa and price_tamarind, respectively.

h. Add three scenarios for those cells with the corresponding names and values for the sales price of each fruit type: Normal season: 450, 820 and 340; Low season: 375, 600 and 310; and High season: 650, 1150 and 500.

i. Play with the scenarios so that you see the Total profit in cell C18 when you have a combination of Worst case for costs and Low season for sales, up to the Best case for costs and High season for sales. Notice that you can't select two scenarios at the same time so you must Click Show individually on each to display them one by one; also, you can see that the Profit by product chart does not automatically change to reflect the different scenarios until you close the Scenario Manager dialog box. Well, back to analyzing your scenarios, you conclude that your business is quite sensitive to these changes in cost and sales price, and that it is not profitable under all scenarios. Now let's add some color to highlight input cells whenever we are using the specified scenarios (by the way, you will now learn a specific conditional formatting trick).

j. Select cells C5:C6, go to Home → Conditional Formatting... → New Rule... → select Use a formula to determine which cells to format → type =AND($C$5=9.5,$C$6=4) in the Format values where this formula is true box, then Click in Format... and select a *light green* as the cell fill in order to represent the Best case scenario for costs (remember values 9.5 and 4.0 were used as the lower costs).

k. Go to your Scenario Manager... button and show the Best case scenario, so your cells C5 and C6 should now be *light green.*

l. Repeat the procedure to make cells C5 and C6 appear with a light yellow fill if the Most likely scenario is selected, and a *light orange* if the Worst case scenario is selected.

m. Repeat the same procedure so that cells C13:E13 appear with the same color scheme for the High season (*light green*), Normal season (*light yellow*) and Low season (*light orange*) (hint: your formula in the Format values where this formula is true box will be similar, based on the =AND( ) logical statement, but will now have three arguments).

n. Before you start playing with your scenarios to check if you got the conditional formatting right, we will add a fantastic, lovely, beautiful and awesome shortcut to the Quick Access Toolbar so that you don't have to access the Scenario Manager... button every time you want to display scenarios. Right Click on the Quick Access Toolbar → Customize Quick Access Toolbar... → select All Commands from the Choose commands from dropdown menu → look for the Scenario command in the list below, select it, Click Add>>, then OK. You should see a new button on your Quick Access Toolbar, and look at what it's got!!! Now it is so easy to display your scenarios. Notice that the Scenario Manager tool just assigns these pre-set values to the corresponding cells; you can still modify these cells manually at any time and recover your scenarios values whenever you want.

o. Ok now you can play with your scenarios as much as you want! If you leave your Most likely cost scenario with the High season price scenario, your SCENARIO MANAGER sheet should look like this (Imperial version not shown, but numbers should be identical):

Buttons used in this step: What-If-Analysis 🔲❓ Conditional Formatting 🔲

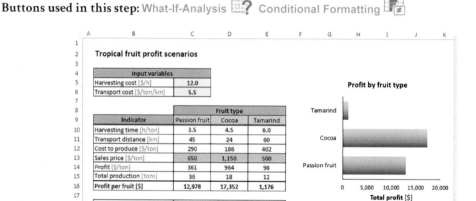

Goal Seek and Solver

As explained in **Section 3.3**, the *Goal Seek* and *Solver* Excel utilities are nothing more than a *What-if Analysis* in reverse order. Let's jump straight into our examples so that you understand their differences:

STEP
16
Goal Seek

a. Go to the GOAL SEEK sheet, which is a car loan calculator. In the Entries section you input the vehicle total price, the down payment and the loan term. There are six options for loan terms, as you can see in cells **F5:F10**, each with a specific interest rate (**G5:G10**). We must use those so, in cell **D6**, apply a *data validation* rule that will only let you choose from the options of cells **F5:F10** (hence a list-based *data validation*).

b. In cell **D8**, use a lookup formula that will automatically retrieve the annual interest rate based on the input of cell **D6**. For example, if 60 months is chosen in cell **D6**, the 1.99 interest rate should appear in cell **D8**.

c. Now you can play with the values in the Entries section and see what happens with the loan in the Results section. Explore the results and make sure you understand what they mean. At the end of the day you are interested in the total amount of money that you pay given your interest rate and, most importantly, your monthly payment. As you play with the input values you are again doing a regular *What-If Analysis*, but have you considered going backwards and, for example, finding out exactly what vehicle price you can afford if you have a budget of $525 per month? You could spend some time trying to get the 525 in cell **D10** by repeatedly changing values in the input cells, but the Goal Seek tool can instantly do this for you.

d. Ok then, let's answer exactly that question. Keeping a 36 loan term and $15,000 down payment, what is the vehicle price (cell D4) that you can afford if you have a monthly budget of $525 (cell D10) to spend on a car? Go to Data → What-If Analysis → Goal Seek..., then enter cell D10 in the Set cell box, type 525 in the To value box and enter cell D4 in the By changing cell box, then stare without blinking your eyes at cell D4 while you Click OK. Do you see what happened? Excel found the car price you can afford so that your monthly payments are $525, which is now displayed in cell D10. If you Click OK in the Goal Seek Status dialog box, the result found will replace the original value of the cell that needed to change (in this case, $33,614.53 will be entered in cell D4); if you press Cancel, the sheet maintains the original value for cell D4; Click OK then.

e. Now, the problem is that with the $33,614.53 you can only afford to buy another sedan, yet an upgrade to a more expensive minivan is inevitable because your family has grown. You still have only $525 for a monthly budget so the loan term needs to be increased in order to get a bigger car. Increase the loan term to 72 months and again run the Goal Seek to see what car price you can afford with a longer term. Wow! It's $50,078.13, which is only a few thousands more than the price of the minivan of your dreams. Done deal! Isn't this incredibly useful? Not as much as pivot tables, but useful!

Buttons used in this step: What-If-Analysis

STEP 17
Solver

a. If you have not installed the Solver add-in, do so now (instructions in **Section 3.3** above). As opposed to the Goal Seek tool, which is limited to one adjustable cell and produces a single solution, the Solver tool can specify multiple adjustable cells and much more as explained in **Section 3.3**. Take, for instance, the following example:

b. Go to the SOLVER sheet, which has a list of production and profit levels for the three tropical fruits of our previous example (actually we are using the same values in previous screenshot); our objective is to define the production in tons so that profit is maximized, but, before you immediately suggest that we should only sell cocoa, which is the most profitable, there are some restrictions that the Solver tool can handle:
   • The combined production capacity for all three fruits is 75 tons per month.
   • 14 tons of tamarind need to be produced every month because a customer that also buys other stuff and is nice to you, needs that order.
   • Your cocoa production is regulated by the ACSTOUCCBR (Association of Centralized Socialist Traditional Organic Unified Cocoa Community Bureau of Regulators), which limits the production of cocoa so that producers do not become too rich and consumers not too fat. The maximum cocoa quota allocated to you is 20 tons per month.
   • Your passion fruit plantations never produce less than 28 tons per month, no matter how lousy a farmer you are.

c. Go to Data → Solver, then enter cell E8 in the Set Objective box and make sure the Max option is chosen, then enter cells C5:C7 in the By Changing Variable Cells box; now specify the constraints by clicking the Add button, then enter cell C8 in the Cell Reference box, select = in the operator menu, and type 75 in the Constraint box, then Click Add.

d. Repeat the same procedure by adding the following restrictions to the list: =$C$7>=14, $C$6<=20 and $C$5>=28; when you are done with the last restriction Click OK instead of Add in the Add Constraint box; select GRG Nonlinear in the Select a Solving Method menu, and Click on the Solve button. Look at how the values in cells C5:C8 now meet our conditions, and when the Solver Results dialog appears, keep the Solver solution and Click OK.

e. Your boss called. She says that the company is increasing capacity to produce a total of 100 tons. Also, the ACSTOUCCBR is now on an indefinite unionized strike because the watchdogs it got to control farmers claim their salary —ironically financed by taxes imposed on cocoa producers— is too low. They also need two more days of vacation every year. Therefore, you can now use your full capacity which is 35 tons of cocoa per month. However, your passion fruit plantations are infested with a plague, so they cannot produce more than 40 tons per month. Input these new conditions in the Solver tool and see the results, which should be:

	Fruit type	Production [tons/month]	Profit [$/ton]	Total profit [$/month]
	Passion fruit	40	361	14,420
	Cocoa	35	964	33,740
	Tamarind	25	98	2,450
	TOTAL	100	-	50,610

Tropical fruit profits

Buttons used in this step: Solver ?↵

Macros

As explained in **Section 3.4**, *macros* involve a sequence of commands that are executed automatically to produce a specific outcome. With *macros* you program Excel to achieve a specific task, but the good news is that you do not need to learn a programming language; instead, you can record a sequence of actions and use a keyboard shortcut to execute them whenever you want. Here you will apply two very simple examples that represent the tip of the iceberg of macros, but that will be enough to demystify this sometimes feared tool and encourage you to take things to the next level.

STEP
18
A very simple macro example

This macro example you are about to do requires a little temporary setting adjustment for it to work, only while it is being recorded.

a.　Go to File → Options → Advanced → uncheck the box for After pressing Enter, move selection, then Click OK. ☐

b.　Go to the MACRO-1 sheet where we will create the simplest of macros that prints the current date as a formatted value in any cell you want. Go to cell B4, then go to the View tab → display the dropdown menu of Macros → Record Macro... → type Current_date in the Macro name box, type capital W in the Ctrl+ box (it should automatically change to Ctrl+Shift+W) and finally Click OK. Your macro is now being recorded so say hi to your webcam and follow the next instructions very carefully while smiling. ☐

c.　In cell B4, type =NOW( ) and press Enter (the cursor should have stayed in that cell) then press Ctrl+C and paste it as value in the same cell B4 (use the Paste Special... button for this); then press Esc to cancel the copy mode. ☐

d.　While in cell B4 (you should have not moved from there) press Ctrl+1 and in the Date format choose the one that displays *Month dd, yyyy* (e.g. March 16, 2014). ☐

e.　Make the cell **bold** and aligned to the left and with font Times New Roman. ☐

f.　Go to the View tab → display the dropdown menu of Macros → Stop Recording. Your macro is ready! If everything went fine in this process, the macro should now work. Let's see: ☐

g.　Go to cell C4 and press Ctrl+Shift+W, which is the shortcut we chose for our macro. You should now see the date in that cell, formatted exactly as in cell B4, except this took you a fraction of a second thanks to the recorded macro. MAGIC! ☐

h. This is so much fun, so go to cell B5 and press Ctrl+Shift+W again, then do it again in cell C5. Did you like your first macro experience?

i. Let's try another simple example: in the same MACROS-1 sheet and starting in cell B8, create a new macro on your own called name that types your full name in font Century Gothic size 16, **bold** and green in any cell by using the shortcut Ctrl+Shift+N.

j. Use this name macro to print your name in cells C8, B9 and C9 (in addition to cell B8 where you recorded your macro).

Buttons used in this step: Macros 🖳

STEP
19
Editing macros

a. Go to the View → Macros → View Macros; there you can visualize all your recorded macros, delete and edit them; this is out of our scope so Click Cancel.

b. Go to File → Options → Advanced → check the After pressing Enter, move selection box so that it is turned back on.

Your MACROS-1 sheet should look like this:

◿	A	B	C	D
1				
2		**Current date & name**		
3				
4		March 16, 2014	March 16, 2014	
5		March 16, 2014	March 16, 2014	
6				
7				
8		Andrés Varhola	Andrés Varhola	
9		Andrés Varhola	Andrés Varhola	
10				

STEP
20
A macro application: fixed reference

a. Go to the MACROS-2 sheet, where you can see a database that shows the top sales of a retail multinational brand across different cities and branches. Each record represents a sale classified as high and achieved by a single sales associate at a particular moment in the year 2013. As the General Manager, you always use this database and you like to sort the records according to different fields, but you need to go back to a specific sorting after you are done with any analysis.

b. Using the filter buttons, sort the records by Sale [CAD$] in descending order (highest to lowest sale), and explore the sales field.

c. Now sort the database according to sales associate from smallest to largest.

d. Sort the database in chronological order of sales (oldest to newest). Now we will record a macro to return the database to sorting by City in ascending order, Branch in ascending order, and Date in ascending order, all at once (instead of doing that every time after you modify the sorting of other columns). Before we do this, we will activate the Developer tab since we will also choose a button to run the macro instead of a keyboard shortcut.

e. If you don't see a Developer tab next to the View tab, go to File → Options → Customize Ribbon → at the right, in the Main Tabs list, check the Developer box so that it is activated, then Click OK.

f. Select cells B4:G72, then go to Developer → Record Macro → call this macro sort in the Macro name box, then type capital S in the Ctrl+ box (Ctrl+Shift+S should now appear), then Click OK.

g. Go to Data → Sort and in the first Sort by box choose City, then Click Add Level, choose Branch # for the Then by box, Add Level again and choose Date in the Then by box, then Click OK.

h. Go to Developer → Click on the Stop Recording button. Let's see if it worked.

i. Sort by Sale [CAD$] in ascending order with the filter button in that column to disrupt our original sorting.

j. Now press Ctrl+Shift+S, which you assigned to our macro in procedure f, and you should now see ☐ the sorting back to City, then Branch # and then Date. Hooray! However, even the Ctrl+Shift+S is too much work in these modern times, so now we will add a button to run the macro.

k. Go to the Developer tab → display the menu under Insert → choose the very first option that ☐ looks like a plain rectangular button; then the mouse cursor becomes a + sign that you will use to draw a button approximately occupying the space of cell F2 (this is a manual exercise) (look at the screenshot below to see what the button looks like). As soon as you are done drawing the button and the Assign Macro box appears, choose the sort macro in the list below to assign it to the button you created; when you see sort in the Macro name box, Click OK.

l. Place the mouse inside the button and edit the text there: type Reset sorting (it may appear as ☐ if your typing is not overwriting the original text, but just keep going) and then go to any cell outside the button (it's ready but DON'T press on it yet). If you are not happy with the size of your button or you want to edit its text, just Right Click on it to select it; then you can delete it or access its contents.

m. Now sort by Sales Associate # in descending order ☐

n. The moment you have been waiting for your entire life has come: press your Reset sorting ☐ button and see what happens. W-O-W, you just created a fancy button that performs a useful and potentially repetitive task.

Buttons used in this step: Record Macro  Sort Stop Recording Insert Controls 🧰

STEP
21
Saving macro-enabled files

Excel uses a different extension for workbooks that contain macros, so:

a. Press Ctrl+S and when the warning appears; you should Click No; then when the Save As dialog ☐ box appears you need to manually choose Excel Macro-Enabled Workbook in the Save as type list, then Click Save. Your filename will now have a **.xlsm** extension instead of the regular **.xlsx**.

The upper part of your MACROS-2 sheet should look like this:

	A	B	C	D	E	F	G	H
1								
2		**2013 top sales database**				Reset sorting		
3								
4		City ▾	Branch ▾	Date ▾	Sale [CAD ▾]	Sales Associat(▾	Shift ▾	
5		Bogotá	7	2013-03-21	$4,720.21	07-006	Morning	
6		Bogotá	7	2013-07-12	$3,588.91	07-003	Afternoon	
7		Bogotá	7	2013-08-11	$3,045.08	07-003	Afternoon	
8		Bogotá	7	2013-10-07	$4,967.97	07-002	Morning	
9		Bogotá	9	2013-01-21	$5,571.64	09-005	Afternoon	
10		Bogotá	9	2013-03-19	$3,791.24	09-008	Afternoon	
11		Bogotá	9	2013-08-18	$5,188.53	09-009	Afternoon	
12		Bogotá	16	2013-01-26	$4,117.67	16-001	Morning	
13		Bogotá	16	2013-03-23	$4,189.74	16-002	Afternoon	
14		Bogotá	16	2013-04-17	$4,339.75	16-003	Afternoon	
15		Bogotá	16	2013-09-15	$4,024.39	16-006	Afternoon	
16		Calgary	10	2013-02-05	$3,952.71	10-007	Afternoon	
17		Calgary	10	2013-02-19	$7,129.34	10-005	Afternoon	
18		Calgary	10	2013-04-20	$3,128.64	10-007	Afternoon	
19		Calgary	15	2013-03-28	$4,080.10	15-001	Morning	

Part B - The ultimate application: producing an error-proof, secure file

You are going to love this exercise: short, concise, merging all your knowledge, showing you a few new tricks, and applicable to a real-life situation.

STEP
01
Open, save and apply data validation

a. Open the file **chapter_07_part_B_ apply_everything.xlsx** and save it in a safe location as **chapter_07_ part_B_apply_everything_solved. xlsx**. Do you remember this file? It is your end product of **Chapter 3, Part C**. Your formulas are there, but consider that this is a file that will be

Figure 21. This guy may be able to destroy his computer, but will never screw up your perfect Excel spreadsheet by overwriting formulas, deleting cells or entering wrong data

used by multiple sales associates, so you need to apply your Excel knowledge to make it secure, protected and error-proof. Here we go!

b. Use the table below to apply the data validation restrictions described there (you must learn on your own how to edit the *error alert styles* and *error messages*):

Column (cells)	Restriction	Error Alert Style	Error message must say:
Invoice (B6:B30)	**Text strings** of exactly 4 characters (because all codes must share the same structure). The invoices should be input with the codes 0001, 0002, etc.	Warning	Invoices must be 4-digit sequential numbers
Type (C6:C30)	**List** based on cells F5:F8 of the PRODUCTS sheet.	Stop	Invalid choice
Product (D6:D30)	**List** that is dependent on what you choose in the Type field. For example, if you select Animal as type, the Product cell to the right must only display options for animals (cells B13:B23 of the PRODUCTS sheet). You must create some names for this to work.	Stop	Invalid choice
Quantity (F6:F30)	**Whole** number between 0 and 100.	Warning	Quantity beyond 0 to 100 or invalid data. Are you sure?
Discount (H6:H30)	**Whole** number between 0 and 60.	Stop	Discount cannot be more than 60%

c. Make sure that your data validation rules work exactly as specified above by entering some data in the applicable fields.

STEP
02
Protecting cells

a. Before we protect your formula cells from being overwritten, let's just type a formula in cells E6:E30 that retrieves the unit price based on the Product column and the prices listed in the PRICE sheet. I am not giving you any hints as to how to do this; you should dominate this by now and if not, check the corresponding answer key file as a last resort (info@excelpro.com).

b. Copy the formats of cells G6:G30 to cells E6:E30, to indicate that we are using a formula there (*Best Practices* rule #10). Ok, now we are ready to protect our cells.

You spent quite a bit of time preparing this beautifully-formatted sheet and someone else will actually enter the new data… To avoid the destruction of your file, we can set it up so that only some cells can be modified. You are interested in protecting your formulas, your title and your headers. In other words, a third-party user should only be allowed to modify cells B6:D30, F6:F30 and H6:H30 (of course in real life you will have many more rows, but this is an example). Now you will learn how to protect the sheet with exceptions.

c.   Select cells B6:D30, F6:F30 and H6:H30 (keep the Ctrl key pressed while selecting non-adjacent cells), then press Ctrl+1 and in the Protection tab, unmark the Locked option to turn it off (cells come locked by default), then Click OK. Nothing happened because we still need to protect the sheet.

d.   Go to the Review tab and Click on the Protect Sheet button, leave the defaults as is in the box that appears and Click OK (notice that you could include a password to unprotect the sheet later, but do not do that now).

e.   Now try to type something in cell E7 or B5 or G20... Realize that you can only type stuff in the cells you determined to be unlocked in procedure c above, and those cells are also supervised by awesome data validation rules. This sheet is so secure that if your cat walked over your keyboard it could only add valid data on it.

f.   Fill in some data invented by you in all the applicable fields (Invoice, Type, Product, Quantity and Discount [%]) so that you experience how nice it is to feel protected by the data validation rules, how easy it is to select a Product from the drop-down menu list, and how the formulas work automatically!

Buttons used in this step: Protect Sheet

STEP
03
Protecting
your file with a
password

Your file is now very functional and good-looking. To add a final touch, we will add a password option so that only authorized people can open it, and that only you, as the General Manager of the Pet Shop, can modify it. I find that option very useful! You do not want your company's sales data visible to everyone in this world.

a.   Go to File → Save As, then choose your safe location and when the Save As dialog box appears, you should see a Tools menu to the left of the Save button in the bottom right. Select this Tools menu → General Options and choose your own Password to open and Password to modify, then Click OK and Save. **Make sure you remember this password** because in Excel there is no easy way to reset it. If you are a student using this book as coursework, you may need to share this password with your teacher for grading purposes, so don't even think about using the password myteacherishorrible77.

b.   Close your file and see what happens when you reopen it. Did your password work? Your file is ready and this book is almost complete. CONGRATULATIONS!!! The next chapter is optional but strongly recommended; if you choose not to complete it for now, please take some time to read the **Final Words** at the end.

5. Review of functions used

=AND( )	**=LEFT( )**
=COUNTA( )	**=NOW( )**
=COUNTIF( )	**=SUM( )**
=INDIRECT( )	**=TODAY( )**
=ISTEXT( )	

CHAPTER 8

Statistical analysis

1. Introduction and learning objectives

This optional chapter is about doing statistical analyses with Excel —which most people believe are exclusive of dedicated statistical software packages. While those programs are indeed more powerful and flexible than Excel when it comes to statistical tools, there are many procedures that you can easily do with our beloved — and sometimes misunderstood and underappreciated— program. Here we will focus on performing *descriptive statistics*, *histograms*, *correlation*, *regression*, and *analysis of variance* (ANOVA), as well as a few functions useful for typical statistical exercises. It is not a pre-requisite to be an expert in Statistics to complete this chapter, nor will you become one after finishing it. Instead, you will benefit from direct and simple applications and interpretations of the most common statistical tests, without formal proofs or deep knowledge of their operation. In other words, you will learn how and when to use the different techniques and how to interpret the results at a very basic, yet practical and useful level.

The learning objectives are:

1. Perform and interpret *descriptive statistics* with the Data Analysis tool.
2. Create histograms with the Data Analysis tool, pivot tables and built-in chart.
3. Perform and interpret *correlation* with the Data Analysis tool.
4. Perform and interpret *regression* with scatter plots.
5. Perform and interpret *analysis of variance* with the Data Analysis tool.

2. Specific Skills

1. **Installing** the Data Analysis tool.
2. **Understanding the components** of the Data Analysis tool, their advantages and limitations.
3. **Understanding statistics** provided by the Descriptive Statistics option of the Data Analysis tool.
4. **Creating *histograms*** with three different procedures: Data Analysis tool, pivot tables and chart (Excel 2016 only).

5. **Understanding *correlation***: identifying when to create a *correlation matrix*; applying conditional formatting to a correlation matrix; interpreting the *Pearson correlation coefficients*.
6. **Understanding *regression***: interpreting the basic outputs of *simple linear regression*: scatter charts, model significance, model coefficients and coefficient of determination.
7. **Understanding one-*way analysis of variance***: applying a *single factor analysis of variance*, and interpreting its results.
8. **Understanding two-*way analysis of variance***: applying a *two factor analysis of variance*, and interpreting its results.
9. **Understanding how to organize data** in order to apply the various statistical tests of interest.

3. Background

3.1 Activating the Data Analysis tool

By default, the Data Analysis tool might not be installed in Excel. If this is the case, follow these steps: File → Options → Add-Ins, select Analysis ToolPak from the list → Go... → Click on the Analysis ToolPak box to turn it on → OK.

You should now see the Data Analysis button at the end of the Data tab.

3.2 Using the Data Analysis tool

The Data Analysis tool is accessed through a button located in the Data → Analysis menu → Data Analysis. You can Click on the Data Analysis button and access a number of options in a list; if you Click on any of those options (e.g. Correlation, Anova: Single Factor, Histogram, etc.), a dialog box appears which firstly requires you to define the location of your data to be analyzed (this means you don't need to select your data before accessing any Data Analysis option). The dialog box will then ask you to specify where you can locate the results, with three possibilities: Output Range (simply any cell within any sheet), New Worksheet Ply (the name of a new sheet you create to receive the output) and a New Workbook (this option creates a new file that you can later save).

One limitation of the Data Analysis tools is that the outputs are static: changing the data will not change the Data Analysis results; if you change the data, the procedure must be repeated. The alternative is to use formulas instead of the Data Analysis, which is initially time-consuming but worth it if data is often updated.

4. Procedures

Through the following steps, you will complete all tasks described in **Section 2**, but not necessarily in the same order. Remember our legend convention as you read: **file name**, Excel location (tab, menu, button, dialog box, control, option or cell coordinates), keyboard or mouse button(s), **formula**, typed data and procedure.

Descriptive Statistics

STEP
01
Open, save and explore

a. Open the file **chapter_08_statistical_analysis.xlsx** and save it in a safe location as **chapter_08_ statistical_analysis_solved.xlsx**. Use the **chapter_08_statistical_analysis_imperial.xlsx** file instead if you wish to work with Imperial units. ☐

b. You will be using the Data Analysis tool quite often for this lab so go to the Data tab → Right Click on the Data Analysis button → Add to Quick Access Toolbar. ☐

c. Go to the DESCRIPTIVE sheet and understand what this database is presenting: a list of more than one thousand baseball players with age, height, weight and waist measurements that we now want to summarize with the Descriptive Statistics tool. Whenever you see a large database like this, immediately ask yourself: What is the average weight? What is the maximum height? Who is the youngest player? What is the difference between the heaviest and the lightest? We will get all that information, which we call descriptive statistics, with a few clicks! ☐

Buttons used in this step: Data Analysis 📊

STEP
02
Descriptive statistics

a. Click on the Data Analysis button that you just added to your Quick Access Toolbar, and choose the Descriptive Statistics option from the Analysis Tools list, then Click OK. ☐

b. Go to the Input Range box and select cells E5:H1039 with your mouse (cell references will be automatically fixed, which is ok), apply the option to show Labels in first row and in the Output Range box type K5 (or simply select cell K5 with the mouse); apply the Summary statistics option and leave all other defaults as is, then Click OK. ☐

c. Auto-adjust the width of columns K to R so that you see our output. ☐

d. The output we got has all the descriptive statistics but is not very elegant since it repeats the statistic name and includes too many decimals. Select cells K5:Q5 and shift them with the mouse one cell to the right, so that they are now occupying cells L5:R5. ☐

e. Select column M and simultaneously (while pressing Ctrl) select columns O and Q; once the three columns are all selected, delete them (Right Click → Delete). ☐

f. Our table headers in the original table are better formatted than the ones generated by the Data Analysis tool, so select cells D5:H5 and copy-paste them onto cells K5:O5, then immediately type Statistic instead of Position in cell K5. ☐

g. Shift cells K7:O19 one row up so that they are now in cells K6:O18. ☐

h. Make all cells in the Descriptive statistics table have one decimal. ☐

i. Some statistics such as the mean, standard deviation, sum, and others, must reflect the same number of decimals as our original data because they are in the same units; however, some statistics like Kurtosis, Skewness and Count, have their own units and may therefore require a different number of decimals. Make all Standard Error, Kurtosis and Skewness data (cells L7:O7 and L12:O13) show 2 decimals, and the Sum and Count data (cells L17:O18) show thousand separators and no decimals. ☐

j. Auto-adjust the width of columns K to O. ☐

STEP
03
Interpreting data

a. Select cells K6, K8:K10 and K14:K17 and make their text **bold**. We highlighted these statistics because they are all in the same unit as the original variable (e.g. years for Age, cm (or in) for Height, etc.). ☐

b. Make sure that you understand what each highlighted statistic means, consulting online if you don't remember. Some fun facts that you can get from the descriptive statistics table are: the average baseball player is very tall (187.2 cm or 6'1"). The tallest is more than 2 m (6'11") high! ☐

The youngest player is almost 21, while the oldest is almost 50; is that possible? Soccer players beyond 35 years old are pretty much done with their career. If you put all these baseball players together, they weigh almost 95 tons (29,714 lb), equivalent to around 20 adult elephants. There are 1,034 players in this database. The most repeated Height value is 188 cm (6.2 ft) and the heaviest player weighs 131.8 kg (290 lb). You see? It's fun.

c. Let's talk a little bit about the *standard deviation*, which is a very important statistic often ignored by most people. Probably the first statistic that we think of when getting some data is the *mean* or *average*, but we rarely think of how variable the data are. For example, two groups of students equally scored 85% on average on a final exam but one group has a very high variability, which means there are very good students but also very bad ones you need to pay more attention to. The standard deviation represents, in simple terms, the average difference between all the records in a variable and the variable's mean. Please find this concept on the Internet, with examples, and make sure you understand it in detail.

Do not worry about statistics not highlighted, as they are beyond the scope of this book. Excel displays them anyway.

STEP
04
Using formulas
to obtain
statistics

You spent some time formatting your table but you saved a lot of time by obtaining it through the Data Analysis button; however, your table is static so if you change your data you must get another table or use formulas. Let's just explain this through a quick example:

a. Select cells E6:E1039 and label them AGE.

b. Go to cell L6 and overwrite the value there with **=AVERAGE(AGE)**. You should have got the same result as before, which was 28.7 years.

c. If you have time, replace other values in your descriptive statistics table with formulas. Most of them you have used before. For standard deviation, the correct function is **=STDEV.P( )** if you measured all the baseball players in what you define as your *population*, which is rarely the case, or **=STDEV.S( )** if you took a *sample* of players from a wider population. For the descriptive statistics table from the Data Analysis tool, Excel uses the sample version by default.

The top of your DESCRIPTIVE sheet should now look like this (screenshot for Imperial units not shown but available in the answer key file):

Human weight and height dataset
Data from *Statistics Online Computational Resource* (SOCR) - www.socr.ucla.edu

Name	Team	Position	Age	Height [cm]	Weight [kg]	Waist [cm]
Adam_Donachie	BAL	Catcher	23.0	188.0	81.8	94.6
Paul_Bako	BAL	Catcher	34.7	188.0	97.7	102.1
Ramon_Hernandez	BAL	Catcher	30.8	182.9	95.5	102.2
Kevin_Millar	BAL	First_Baseman	35.4	182.9	95.5	87.9
Chris_Gomez	BAL	First_Baseman	35.7	185.4	85.5	98.9
Brian_Roberts	BAL	Second_Baseman	29.4	175.3	80.0	80.8
Miguel_Tejada	BAL	Shortstop	30.8	175.3	95.0	102.3
Melvin_Mora	BAL	Third_Baseman	35.1	180.3	90.9	87.4
Aubrey_Huff	BAL	Third_Baseman	30.2	193.0	105.0	107.9
Adam_Stern	BAL	Outfielder	27.1	180.3	81.8	92.2
Jeff_Fiorentino	BAL	Outfielder	23.9	185.4	85.5	99.8
Freddie_Bynum	BAL	Outfielder	27.0	185.4	81.8	83.2
Nick_Markakis	BAL	Outfielder	23.3	188.0	84.1	97.7
Brandon_Fahey	BAL	Outfielder	26.1	188.0	72.7	82.9
Corey_Patterson	BAL	Outfielder	27.6	175.3	81.8	103.2

Statistic	Age	Height [cm]	Weight [kg]	Waist [cm]
Mean	28.7	187.2	91.7	98.1
Standard Error	0.13	0.18	0.30	0.25
Median	27.9	188.0	90.9	97.8
Mode	24.9	188.0	90.9	101.3
Standard Deviation	4.3	5.9	9.6	7.9
Sample Variance	18.7	34.3	91.2	62.1
Kurtosis	0.55	0.35	0.21	0.57
Skewness	0.86	0.22	0.36	0.30
Range	27.6	40.6	63.6	62.0
Minimum	20.9	170.2	68.2	75.6
Maximum	48.5	210.8	131.8	137.6
Sum	29,714	193,556	94,812	101,468
Count	1,034	1,034	1,034	1,034

Histograms

The *descriptive statistics* procedure is the first step you undertake after you collect some data. However, it is also very important to visualize how these data are distributed. You may know that the average weight of your baseball players is 91.7 kg (201.7 lb) with a standard deviation of 9.6 kg (21 lb), a minimum of 68.2 kg (150 lb) and a maximum of 131.8 kg (290 lb), but a histogram will show you a graphical representation of the entire distribution of this variable. Do we have many players that are heavy and a few that are light? Are most players close to the average and only a few in the extremes?

Visualizing the frequency distribution of variables (i.e. creating *histograms*) is an important part of data analysis. While the Data Analysis tool has the option to create a histogram, doing it from pivot tables is much better since the histograms will remain connected to your data. You will now see the difference between both procedures.

STEP
05
Histogram
from Data
Analysis tool

a. Go to the DESCRIPTIVE sheet and press the Data Analysis button → Histogram → OK then select cells G6:G1039 for the Input Range, leave the Bin Range box empty, type HISTOGRAM-UGLY in the New Worksheet Ply box, and include the Chart Output option before pressing OK. You can see that Excel automatically defined the class widths of your histogram since we did not input a range of cells with our own class bins in the Bin Range box. Also, the default histogram is ugly with so many decimals. Some statisticians say that histograms should not have gaps between their frequency columns, but you see how Excel does not follow that rule by default. Next, we will use pivot tables and charts to produce better histograms. ☐

STEP
06
Histogram
from a pivot
table

a. Go to the DESCRIPTIVE sheet and select cells E5:H1039, then Insert → Pivot Table → OK; when the new sheet appears drag the Weight [kg] (Weight [lb]) field to the Rows quadrant. ☐

b. Right Click on any cell of the first column of the pivot table (column A) → Group... → type 0 in the Starting at box and Click OK. ☐

c. Drag the Weight [kg] (Weight [lb]) field to the Values quadrant. Make sure the pivot table is counting the data instead of summing them. ☐

d. Add a column to the left of your pivot table and another row on top, hide the gridlines and type Weight distribution on cell B2, making that cell **bold** and size 14. ☐

e. Label your sheet HISTOGRAMS-NICE. ☐

f. Create a column pivot chart from your table and make it look good (remember that a histogram must not have gaps between columns). ☐

g. In the same sheet, create more pivot tables and charts for the Age, Height [m] (Height [ft]) and Waist [cm] (Waist [in]), adding titles for each table as you did for cell B2 (at this point look at the screenshot below to get the idea of what we want). Use your criteria so that the histograms make sense, especially regarding the range of each class. Some statisticians argue that a proper histogram should not have less than five classes and no more than twenty. ☐

h. Interpret your histograms and make sure that you understand their utility, and how they complement the descriptive statistics. ☐

Buttons used in this step: Pivot Table

Your HISTOGRAMS sheet should look like this (table formats and exact location of tables and charts don't matter) (screenshot for Imperial units not shown, but available in the answer key file):

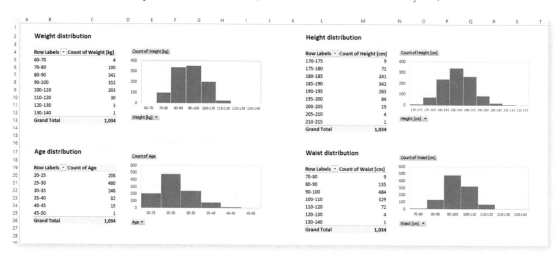

STEP

07

OPTIONAL: Histogram chart with Excel 2016

a. If you have Excel® 2016 installed, put the cursor on any cell of the Age field of the DESCRIPTIVE sheet and then go to Insert → Recommended Charts → go to the All Charts tab and select Histogram, then Click OK. Note that not all Excel® 2016 versions may have this option.

b. Make the graph comprehensive by changing the title to Age distribution, add a horizontal axis title saying Age [years] and a vertical axis title saying Frequency. Also get rid of the chart border but add a light gray border to the Plot Area. (when are they going to fix that default issue?).

c. Note how this first attempt of a histogram is very decent. Still, we can also modify the category ranges for age. Right Click on the *x-axis* scale → Format Axis... → Axis Options, and then play with the Bin width, Number of bins, Overflow bin and Underflow bin boxes to understand what they do. You may return to the Automatic option at the end, although the Overflow bin appears useful for this example. Note that a limitation with this built-in chart option is that we cannot manually set up the starting point for the first category, which would allow us to display whole numbers. With pivot table-derived histograms it was feasible, but we needed to spend a bit more time creating the graph. Also, I am not sure I like the parentheses in the categories for the graph you just created. Nothing is perfect! Your chart should look like this:

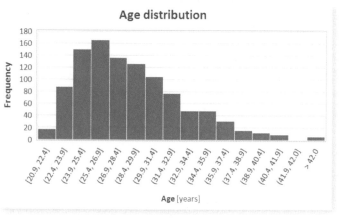

Buttons used in this step: Recommended Charts

Correlation

a. Go to the CORRELATION sheet and analyze the data presented; it shows some indicators by country and we want to analyze the relationship between those indicators (you may want to find out what GDP is on the Internet, if you don't know). For example, you might be interested in knowing if higher CO_2 *emissions per capita reduce infant mortality rate* (they do! CO_2 also happens to be plant food), or if increasing education expenditure results in more Nobel laureates. But why not check the correlation between all variables at the same time to identify interesting relationships? Let's see how we can do that:

b. Press the Data Analysis button and choose Correlation from the list → OK; in the dialog that appears select cells C6:O145 for the Input Range, Click on Labels in first row, select New Worksheet Ply and type COUNTRY MATRIX in the box next to it, then Click OK.

c. Go to the COUNTRY MATRIX sheet that was just created and do all you need to do to make it look like the screenshot provided below (consider gridlines, table borders, number of decimals, alignment, subscript in CO_2, etc.).

d. Select cells C5:O17 and apply a conditional formatting that resembles the screenshot below.

Your COUNTRY MATRIX sheet should look like this:

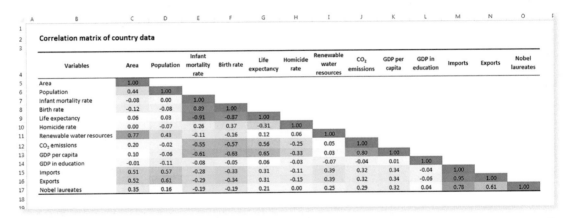

Variables	Area	Population	Infant mortality rate	Birth rate	Life expectancy	Homicide rate	Renewable water resources	CO_2 emissions	GDP per capita	GDP in education	Imports	Exports	Nobel laureates
Area	1.00												
Population	0.44	1.00											
Infant mortality rate	-0.08	0.00	1.00										
Birth rate	-0.12	-0.08	0.89	1.00									
Life expectancy	0.06	0.03	-0.91	-0.87	1.00								
Homicide rate	0.00	-0.07	0.26	0.37	-0.31	1.00							
Renewable water resources	0.77	0.43	-0.11	-0.16	0.12	0.06	1.00						
CO_2 emissions	0.20	-0.02	-0.55	-0.57	0.56	-0.25	0.05	1.00					
GDP per capita	0.10	-0.06	-0.61	-0.63	0.65	-0.33	0.03	0.80	1.00				
GDP in education	-0.01	-0.11	-0.08	-0.05	0.06	-0.03	-0.07	-0.04	0.01	1.00			
Imports	0.51	0.57	-0.28	-0.33	0.31	-0.11	0.39	0.32	0.34	-0.04	1.00		
Exports	0.52	0.61	-0.29	-0.34	0.31	-0.15	0.39	0.32	0.34	-0.06	0.95	1.00	
Nobel laureates	0.35	0.16	-0.19	-0.19	0.21	0.00	0.25	0.29	0.32	0.04	0.78	0.61	1.00

Correlation matrix of country data

a. Go to your COUNTRY MATRIX sheet and look at your data. The numbers you see in your correlation matrix are called *Pearson correlation coefficients* (r) and work like this: a value of 1.00 indicates a perfect direct positive linear relationship between variables (i.e. as one increases the other one increases, with no scatter between them). A value of -1.00 indicates a direct negative linear relationship (i.e. as one decreases the other one increases, with no scatter). A value of 0 means absolutely no relationship between the variables. The closer the *Pearson correlation coefficient* is to 1 or -1, the higher the correlation between the variables. The conditional formatting we applied is very useful when looking at correlation matrices; however, you must always remember that a correlation matrix is an exploratory tool, as correlation does not necessarily mean causation. Sometimes variables are highly correlated by chance and not through a meaningful physical relationship between them.

b. Look at your correlation coefficients and focus your attention on the highest absolute values (bluer or redder) to detect any interesting relationship. Do they all make sense or are there unexpected results? (e.g. why is the number of *Nobel laureates* not correlated with *GDP in education* and highly correlated with *Imports* and *Exports*?). If you find a high correlation, it is also important to be able to explain which variable is the cause and which variable is the effect. For example, there is a high correlation between CO_2 *emissions* and *GDP per capita* (r = 0.80). Which one drives which and why? Just think about it.

Regression

As you may know already, *regression* is a technique to produce models that predict one unknown dependent variable based on the value of a known *independent variable*; this is possible if you have a good dataset with accurate measurements of both variables. For example, when you measure trees in the field, tree height is difficult and time consuming to obtain; therefore, you may want to be able to predict height based on diameter, which is very easy and quick to measure. Simple linear regression, which is indeed the simplest form of regression, is based on models with this structure:

$$y = a + bx$$

Where *y* is the dependent variable to be predicted, *x* is the independent variable or predictor, and *a* (*intercept*) and *b* (*slope*), also known as *model coefficients*, are constants whose values are found by applying the linear regression techniques. There are other types of model structures but they always have a *y* that needs to be predicted based on *x*. While fitting regression models is subject to several statistical rules and assumptions, here you will learn the basics of how to use Excel to generate these models. There are two ways to do it: 1) through *scatter charts* and 2) with the Regression option within the Data Analysis tool. The advantage of the first one is that you can apply various types of models (linear, exponential, logarithmic, etc.), but you cannot analyze the models to determine if their coefficients and the model as a whole are statistically significant. The advantage of using the Data Analysis tool for regression is that it does tell you if the model is statistically significant and automatically shows the distribution of residuals to help you detect potential bias; however, you can only apply simple linear models like the one described above. In this chapter we will only review the use of regression through scatter plots, and we will leave the Data Analysis tool option for another occasion.

STEP
10
Regression
with scatter
charts

a.   Go to the REGRESSION sheet and look at the data presented there; we basically show analogous data for trees and humans: tree diameter (measured at 1.3 m or 4 ft above the ground) is equivalent to human waist circumference, tree height is equivalent to human height and tree volume is analogous to human weight. We measured 170 individuals of both trees and humans (the latter, by the way, were extracted randomly from the data in the DESCRIPTIVE sheet). ☐

b.   Let's create a first tree chart: select cells **C4:D175** and go to Insert → Scatter chart (first option) (recall **Chapter 5**). ☐

c.   Make this graph look nice and complete, adding proper axis names, removing decimals, typing a comprehensive title and anything appealing to your exquisite taste (I will, for example, use the same marker color as the headers for each table: green for trees and blue for humans). I will only suggest a title that you will later edit in other graphs: Tree diameter - height relationship. ☐

d.   Right Click on the chart → Add Trendline, then keep the Linear option and turn on the Display Equation on chart and Display R-squared value on chart options; also Click on the Custom option for the Trendline Name but leave the box blank. ☐

e.   Move the trendline box within the chart elsewhere if it is overlapping with the data, and format the trendline so that it is thicker and stands out from the data points (you can do this with Right Click over the trendline). ☐

f.   **Understand the following**: the R^2 value displayed in the box is called the *coefficient of determination*, which is mathematically equivalent to the square of the *Pearson correlation coefficient* that describes the relationship between the variables (remember correlation above?). R^2 can vary from 0.00, when a relationship between two variables does not exist, to 1.00, where there is a perfect relationship with no variation in the data. ☐

g.   Now copy and paste this chart so that you create an identical copy below it, and edit everything so that it now shows the relationship between tree diameter and volume (with diameter always in the *x-axis*). ☐

h.   As soon as you create the tree diameter - volume graph, you notice that the linear trendline is not a very good fit with the data points. Right Click on this trendline, select Format Trendline... ☐

and explore the different model types (Exponential, Logarithmic, etc.). Choose the one that maximizes R^2 as displayed in your chart.

i.   Now create a third chart that shows the best trendline for the relationship between tree height and tree volume (height on the *x-axis* and volume on the *y-axis*). ☐

j.   Create the three equivalent charts for humans; you can play around to explore different model types and their effect on R^2, but in the end please choose a linear model for all human graphs. Make sure that you edit the axis scales in the human graphs so that you see the data variation properly. For example, the waist axis can go from 80 to 120 cm (30 to 50 in) because if it starts at 0, the data points will show as a small cloud in the corner. ☐

Buttons used in this step: Insert Scatter

Your graphs should look like the ones below; I don't know about you, but trees make more sense than humans to me (Imperial unit version screenshot not shown, but available in the answer key file):

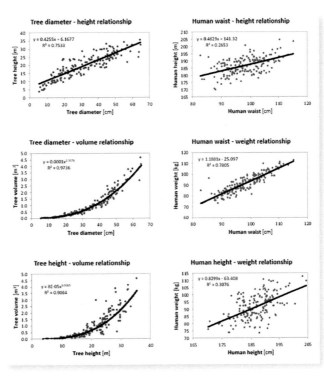

STEP

11

Applying regression

Your graphs look very nice, but do you know how to use them? We will now type formulas in cells **N3** and **O3** to predict tree height and volume, respectively, from any diameter value, and then do the same for humans.

a.   If you are using metric units, go to cell **N3** and type =IF(M3<>"",0.4255*M3+6.1677,"-"). For Imperial units, the formula should be =IF(M3<>"",3.5455*M3+20.235,"-"). Look at your graphs below to understand where we got the formula for the second argument of this *IF* statement. ☐

b.   Type 45 in cell **M3** if using metric or 18 if using Imperial. According to your regression model, a *Pinus radiata* tree with 45 cm (18 in) in trunk diameter will have a height of 25.3 m (84.1 ft). Remember that this is a central estimate that will not necessarily be accurate because there are always natural variations, as shown by the scatter in your graphs. ☐

c.   Type a formula in cell **O3** that will predict tree volume based on the diameter input on cell **M3**. Use the same structure and logic as the N3 formula. Your 45 cm (18 in) tree should have a volume of 1.40 m³ (59.3 ft³). ☐

d.   Repeat the procedure to complete cell S3, which should produce a value of 93.7 kg (203.7 lb) for a waist of 100.0 cm (39 in). Do you wonder why we don't even try to predict human height based on waist? Because that model with an R^2 of 0.27 is a total disaster.

Important disclaimer: *regression* is an extensive topic studied in dedicated term-long Statistics courses; to officially perform regression you must make sure a number of requirements not discussed in this chapter are met. Here you have just briefly learned some basic aspects of this technique and the main purpose was to show how it is done in Excel.

One-way analysis of variance (ANOVA)

On your own, browse the internet to understand what ANOVA is if you don't know already, before going through the following steps. Then go to the 1-WAY ANOVA sheet, where this exercise is proposed: *Canada's primary agricultural regions for growing fruits, including grapes for wine, require ample annual precipitation. Shown below is annual precipitation, in millimeters, for select communities in each region. At ∝ = 0.05, is there sufficient evidence to indicate a difference in the mean precipitation for the regions?*

STEP

12

One-way
ANOVA

a.   Go to the 1-WAY ANOVA sheet and Click on the Data Analysis tool → highlight Anova: Single Factor → OK then select cells B4:D9 for the Input Range, select the Labels in First Row box, leave Alpha as 0.05 and select cell F4 for the Output Range, then Click OK. If you wish, get rid of the extra decimals that appear in the tables that Excel generated automatically.

b.   **Interpret the results**: if the *F* value shown in cell J15 is larger than the *F crit* value of cell L15, then there you can conclude, with 95% confidence (since *alpha* was 0.05), that at least one of the group means is significantly different from the others. The *P-value* of cell K15 also points to that conclusion but is even more precise: it is the probability of making a mistake by saying that at least one group mean is different from the others. Note that we got a very small number so thus it is virtually impossible to make a mistake by saying that there are differences in precipitation for at least one location. ANOVA does not tell you which group is different from which; for that you have to apply another test which is out of the scope of this book.

c.   Make the value of cell K15 red (font color), since this is the key value that summarizes our ANOVA (this way you will never forget what to look at first when interpreting the results of ANOVA). Your sheet should look like this (Imperial unit version not shown, but *P-value* should be identical to the one in red below):

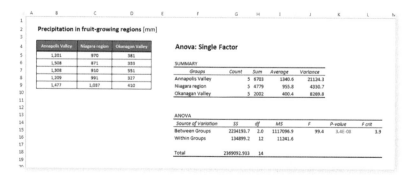

Two-way analysis of variance (ANOVA)

The previous exercise was applied to a case with one factor (precipitation). In a two-way analysis of variance, you can establish differences between groups when two factors are applied; the following example shows such a case: *A company sells three items: swimming pools, spas, and saunas. The owner decides to see whether the age of the sales representative and the type of item affect monthly sales. At $\propto$ = 0.05, analyze the data shown, using a two-way ANOVA. Sales are given in hundreds of dollars for a randomly selected month, and five salespeople were selected for each group.**

STEP
13
Two-way
ANOVA

a. Go to the 2-WAY ANOVA sheet and Click on the Data Analysis button → Anova Two-Factor With Replication → OK, then select cells B4:E14 while in the Input Range box, type 5 in the Rows per sample box, leave Alpha at 0.05 and select cell G4 for the Output Range. ☐

b. Change the font color of cells L28:L30 to red, to remind you what the most important results ☐ of this analysis are.

c. **Interpret the results**: the interpretation of *F* and *F crit* values as well as *P-values* shown in cells ☐ K28:M30 is the same as with the one-way ANOVA (read step above again if necessary). In this exercise, the *P-value* larger than 0.05 in cell L28 suggests that there is a relatively high probability of error if one concludes that there is a statistical difference between the means of the two age groups (Over 30 and 30 or under) when analyzed independently. On the other hand, the low *P-value* of cell L29 confirms that there are statistically significant differences in sales between products (Pool, Spa and Sauna), when analyzed independently. Finally, cell L30 reveals a statistically-significant interaction between the two factors (age and product type); this means that while there were no differences in sales between the two age groups when considering all products as a whole, a specific age group might be better at selling a specific type of product (e.g. maybe people over 30 love saunas and might therefore close more deals for that product).

Your 2-WAY ANOVA sheet should look like this:

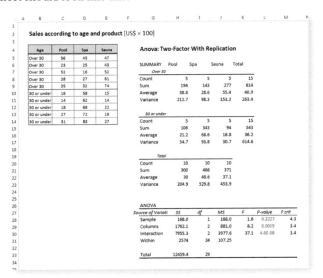

Congratulations! You have finished this book! Please take a couple of minutes to read the **Final words & indices** section next, and remember to use Excel for everything from now on.

* Bluman A.G. & Mayer J.G. 2011. Elementary Statistics - A Step by Step Approach. Second Canadian Edition. McGraw-Hill, Canada. 762 p.

5. Review of functions used

=AVERAGE( )   =IF( )   =STDEV.S( )

Final words and indices

I hope that your life has changed by completing this book. From now on, it is of great importance that every time you face a task where Excel could help, you use it. Think Excel, breathe Excel and do Excel, for a skill must be exercised constantly to be preserved and improved. Besides learning the technical aspects of our lovely program, whether it is writing a complex formula or changing the layout of a chart, reading this book also taught you the culture of producing highly professional spreadsheets with good-looking interfaces, error-proof functionalities and, above all, full automation. Please review and apply our **Best Practices** every time you work with Excel, and take some time to visit `www.excelpro.com` for news and updates about the **Excelling in Life** publications.

Further reading and training

Now that you are an advanced Excel user, please consult online or in the literature about any specific trick that you require if not shown in this book. The internet is full of free forums, tutorials, videos, blogs and published books that will let you find virtually every answer. I find the **Excel Bible** series by John Walkenbach extremely comprehensive and worth having in your bookshelf if you constantly use the program, as encouraged by completing this book. Having done so means that you have opened the door to computer programming. If you want to further explore more complex macros or sophisticated coding in the environment in which Excel works, pursue learning Visual Basic. Finally, stay tuned at `www.excelpro.com`.

Function index

=PI( ): 52
=PROPER( ): 33
=RANK( ): 40
=REPLACE( ): 33
=REPT( ): 33, 121, 122
=RIGHT( ): 33, 41, 43, 121, 122
=ROUND( ): 14, 15, 17, 121, 122
=ROUNDDOWN( ): 37
=ROWS( ): 47
=SEARCH( ): 33, 34
=SECOND( ): 38
=STDEV.P( ): 112
=STDEV.S( ): 112

=SUBSTITUTE( ): 33, 34
=SUM( ): 9, 14, 15, 26, 49, 99, 123, 124
=SUMIF( ): 43, 49, 50, 58, 87, 121, 122
=SUMIFS( ): 49, 50
=TEXT( ): 33, 38, 88
=TIME( ): 38
=TODAY( ): 24, 36, 38, 97
=TRIM( ): 33
=UPPER( ): 33
=VLOOKUP( ): 61, 63, 64, 66, 121, 122
=WEEKDAY( ): 38, 42, 88
=WORKDAY( ): 38
=YEAR( ): 38

Select formula index

Some key formulas used throughout the book have been selected to be part of the following index and detailed explanation, to help the readers understand them. The criteria for selecting formulas for this index were: relatively complex, of potential common use, interesting logic and not already explained in detail in the book. The following table shows the location of those formulas in the book by **Chapter** (Ch.), **Part**, **Step** and **Procedure** (Proc.), as well as the file, sheet and example of a cell where the formula is applied after completing all the steps in each chapter. In the **Select formula explanation** section below, there is a written decription of the logic behind the formulas and the outputs they produce. Both tables are linked through the number in their first columns.

No.	Ch.	Part	Step	Proc.	File, Sheet - example cell*	Original formula
1	1	A	14	e	chapter_01_part_A_sales DATA - G2	=ROUND(C5*$G$2,0)
2	1	A	16	f	chapter_01_part_A_sales DATA - D4	=AVERAGE(C$9:C$371)
3	1	B	6	c	chapter_01_part_B_top_customers TOP CUSTOMERS - H9	=IF(D6="New York",G6/0.90,G6)
4	2	A	5	d	chapter_02_part_A_text TEXT - C6	=REPT(CHAR(110),B6/10)
5	2	D	6	c	chapter_02_Part_D_installation_hours WORK HOURS - P2	=SUMIF($A$7:$A$77,RIGHT(O2,1),$O$7:$O$77)
6	3	A	7	a	chapter_03_part_A_count_and_sum CONDITIONAL SUMMING - K5	=SUMIF(H5:H1555,"Martin",G5:G1555)
7	4	A	2	a	chapter_04_part_A_lookup VLOOKUP-exact - H5	=VLOOKUP($H$4,$B$5:$E$12,2,FALSE)
8	4	A	5	a	chapter_04_part_A_lookup BEST LOOKUP - I6	=INDEX(B$5:B$13,MATCH(I$4,F$5:F$13,0))

* This cell reference is a single example where the formula is applied in the finished solved files; this example reference may not coincide with the references in the original formula listed in the last column of this table due to changes applied after the step and procedure where the formula was first introduced. For example, formula 2 above references cells C$9:C$371 but ends up in column D after completing some steps, hence a sample cell where you find it in the completed file is D4 of the DATA sheet in the file **chapter_01_part_A_sales**.

Select formula explanation

No.	Column (cells)	Explanation
1	=ROUND(C5*$G$2,0)	The first argument of this formula, C5*$G$2, simply invokes a number that will be displayed with no decimals, as determined by the second argument 0. If the formula is copied elsewhere, the fixed reference in cell G2 will prevent it from moving.
2	=AVERAGE(C$9:C$371)	The formula calculates the arithmetic average of numerical data included in cells C9:C371; if non-numerical data are within that range, the function will ignore them. The formula will change the column references if copied sideways but will stay on rows 9 to 371 if copied upwards or downwards.
3	=IF(D6="New York",G6/0.90,G6)	A beautiful and very useful IF statement, this formula divides the value in cell G6 by 0.90 (second argument) if the content of cell D6 is New York (first argument); if the content of D6 is not New York, it simply displays the value of cell G6 (third argument).
4	=REPT(CHAR(110),B6/10)	The first argument of this formula uses the =CHAR( ) function to invoke character #110 of the computer's character code, which corresponds to the letter n. The second argument repeats this character a specified number of times, in this case the number input in cell B6 divided by 10. If applied with a regular font and if 100 is input in cell B6, the formula will produce a text string showing the letter n ten times. In the example of **Chapter 2**, the font *Wingdings* is applied to the cell where the formula is written, therefore showing the symbol ■ instead of letter n.
5	=SUMIF($A$7:$A$77,RIGHT(O2,1),$O$7:$O$77)	This formula is adding up the numerical data in cells O7:O77 (third argument) but only if the first character to the right in cell O2 is found in the corresponding cells in the A7:A77 range. For example, if CREW-1 is input in cell O2, 1 is only a unique value in cells A8, A10 and A70, and cells O8, O10 and O70 all contain values of 10, the formula output will be 30. Changing the value of cell A8 to 2 would change the formula output to 20. Changing the value of cell O10 to 20 would result in 40.
6	=SUMIF(H5:H1555,"Martin",G5:G1555)	The formula will add all numerical values within cells G5:G1555 if Martin is in the same rows of column H.
7	=VLOOKUP($H$4,$B$5:$E$12,2,FALSE)	This formula will look for the value entered in cell H4 (first argument) within the cells in the first column of the B5:E12 range (column B or cells B5:B12), and will retrieve the value of the second column (third argument) in the same line where the value of cell H4 was found in cells B5:B12). For example, if A was input in cell H4 and found for the first time in cell B8, the formula would return the contents of cell C8.
8	=INDEX(B$5:B$13,MATCH(I$4,F$5:F$13,0))	This formula is shown here with cell references instead of names, which are applied in the example of **Chapter 4**. The MATCH(I$4,F$5:F$13,0) part retrieves the position in which the value of cell I4 is located within cells F5:F13. For example, if the text USA is in cell I4 and first appears in cell F6, the result of this part of the formula would be 2 (second position within the F5:F13 range). The third argument of =MATCH, here 0, specifies that an exact value is being looked up (USA and only USA). The first argument of the =INDEX function indicates the cell range within which you want to retrieve a value, and the second argument, in this case entirely filled by the MATCH(I$4,F$5:F$13,0)), the position where the value should be retrieved. Following our USA example supposedly appearing in cells I4 and F6, the result of the entire formula would be the value of cell B6. To summarize, the formula is looking for USA in column F and retrieving the value in the same row of column B. The example in the book applies to cars, but the idea is the same.

Glossary of terms

Argument. Component of a function; for example, the **=IFERROR( )** function has two arguments: *value* and *value if error*. See also: *function*.

Array. Group of contiguous cells, also known as *range*.

Conditional formatting. Procedure in Excel that allows the user to allocate a specific format to a cell given its contents or the contents of other cells; for example, you can make an entire row appear light blue if one of its cells contains a specific value.

Data validation. Procedure applied to restrict what you can enter in a specific cell or group of cells; for example, you may want to allow whole numbers from 1 to 100 to your teaching assistants grading your student assignments.

Database. Records ordered in a highly structured group of cells that include a single row header with clear field descriptions. For example, a table that shows a list of last names, first names, telephone numbers and gender. Proper databases are required to produce pivot tables and charts. See also: *range, table, field, relational database*.

Field. A single column in a database, which refers to a characteristic of the records in the database. For example, a database of customers might have their name, address and phone number as three fields. See also: *database, record*.

Fixed reference. Reference cells within a function or formula that, if copied elsewhere, will not change the location of these cells, specified by the $ symbol. For example, the formula **=SUM($A$1:$A$10)** will remain identical if copied to a different cell. See also: *relative reference, semi-relative reference*.

Function. Built-in command that performs a specific task in Excel. For example, **=COUNT( )** is a function that counts the number of values in a user-defined cell range which constitutes its only argument. See also: formula, argument.

Formula. A mathematical or logical expression to perform a specific operation, which may or may not include a function. For example, **=A1*A5/SUM(B4:B8)** is a formula that contains one function while **=A1-B5*C8^D4** has no functions.

Goal Seek. Excel tool that allows you to get the input value you require for a formula to produce the desired result. See also: *Solver*.

Macro. A set of commands automatically run once the user has defined them. For example, a macro can be used to execute repetitive tasks such as applying a complex formatting to a cell (blue, bold font with borders) in a single step.

Name: a user-defined alphanumeric code that identifies a specific value, a cell or a group of cells. For example, the formula **=SUM(A1:A10)** can become **=SUM(SALES)** by labeling cells **A1:A10** as **SALES**.

Pivot chart. The graphic representation of a *pivot table*.

Pivot table. An automated and dynamic tabular report that summarizes specific aspects of a database as designed by the user. For example, from a list of daily sales, a pivot table could show the sum of sales per month or year. See also: *pivot chart*.

Range. Group of contiguous cells. See also: *table, array*.

Record. Single row of a database, which contains the information of a unique subject in the database. For example, a database of customers might have their name, address, credit card information, etc. An individual customer constitutes a record of that database. See also: *database, field*.

Relative reference. Referenced cells within a function or formula that, if copied elsewhere, will accordingly change those references. For example, if the formula =**SUM(A1:A10)** in cell A11 is copied to cell B11, it will become =**SUM(B1:B10)**. See also: *fixed reference, semi-relative reference*.

Relational database. A database linked to another through at least one common field. For example, in one database you can see identification number, last name, first name and telephone number, while in another you see identification number, favorite TV show and weight. See also: *database, field, record*.

Scenario Manager. A tool that allows you to store pre-defined values to be entered in specific cells as required.

Semi-relative reference. Referenced cells within a function or formula that, if copied elsewhere, will partly change. For example, if the formula =**SUM(A$1:A$10)** in cell A11 is copied to cell A12, it will remain the same; but if copied to cell B12 it will become =**SUM(B$1:B$10)**. See also: *fixed reference, semi-relative reference*.

Solver. Tool that allows you to define the multiple input values required to produce a desired outcome in a formula, given possible restrictions. See also: *Goal Seek*.

Spreadsheet. An electronic document consisting of a grid of cells where inputs and outputs can be generated. See also: *worksheet, workbook*.

Table. A formatted range of cells, which in Excel automates certain tasks. See also: *range*.

Text string. A combination of one or more alphanumeric and numeric characters put together continuously in a single cell. A text string may contain letters, numbers or special symbols.

Workbook. A group of *worksheets* in a single Excel file.

Worksheet. A single spreadsheet in Excel, consisting of columns and rows. See also: *spreadsheet, workbook*.

Figure credits

Figure	Licensed source	Author or copyright holder
Page xii	Adobe Stock	WavebreakMediaMicro
Page xvi	fotoarkitekt.com	Gonzalo Villota, Varhola Productions
Page xviii	Bigstock by Shutterstock	morganlstudios
Figure 3	Adobe Stock	Николай Татару
Figure 4	Bigstock by Shutterstock	gjohnstonphoto
Page 28	fotoarkitekt.com	Gonzalo Villota, Varhola Productions
Figure 6	Bigstock by Shutterstock	andy0man
Figure 7	Adobe Stock	elnur
Figure 8	Adobe Stock	Carsten Reisinger
Page 44	fotoarkitekt.com	Gonzalo Villota, Varhola Productions
Figure 9	Bigstock by Shutterstock	ollirg
Figure 10	Adobe Stock (adapted)	Graphithèque
Figure 11	Adobe Stock (adapted)	Kamadja
Page 55	Adobe Stock (adapted)	burak duman
Figure 13	Bigstock by Shutterstock	PongMoji
Figure 15	Google Earth	---
Figure 16	Bigstock by Shutterstock	frbird
Figure 17	Bigstock by Shutterstock	vikea
Figure 18	Bigstock by Shutterstock	Wavebreak Media Ltd
Figure 19	Adobe Stock	Daniel Ernst
Figure 21	Bigstock by Shutterstock	auremar